HOW TO ... HOW TO ... HOW TO ...

run a quality
bed + breakfast

Published by VisitBritain, Thames Tower, Blacks Road, London W6 9EL
Publishing Manager: Seth Edwards
Production Manager: Celine Gale
Written by: Christopher Howard and David Falk at East of
England Tourist Board
Typesetting: Keystroke, Jacaranda Lodge, Wolverhampton
Printing and binding: Wace Ltd, Swindon
Cover design: Eugenie Dodd Typographics

Front cover image courtesy of britainonview.com

Important note: the information contained in this publication has been
published in good faith on the basis of information submitted to VisitBritain.
Whilst every effort has been made to ensure that this information is correct,
VisitBritain regrets that it cannot guarantee complete accuracy and all liability
for loss, disappointment, negligence or other damages caused by reliance
on the information contained in this publication, is hereby excluded. As
changes often occur after press date, it is advisable to confirm the
information given.

ISBN – 0-7095-8277-3

visit **Britain**
publishing

Contents

Chapter 1
First thoughts

Running a bed and breakfast (B&B) is extremely rewarding, enjoyable and varied, but it is not an easy option; it requires commitment, energy and enthusiasm, and it can be *very* busy indeed. Before you embark on a decision that will have a huge effect on your life and the lives of those around you, you will need to be sure that running a B&B is the right thing for you to do.

This chapter will give you an idea of what is involved in running a B&B, and of what questions you should ask yourself before you decide to go ahead. At the end of it, you should know whether a B&B is right for you and you should be in a better position to make your decision.

Is running a B&B the right thing for you to do?

This section deals with the advantages and disadvantages of running a B&B, and with what you should consider before you make your decision. It also challenges many of the misconceptions about running a B&B, and uses case studies to help you decide whether running a B&B is really the right step for you to take.

COPING WITH THE COMMITMENT AND THE CHANGE IN LIFESTYLE

Running a B&B may have been a long-term plan for you or the result of a change in personal circumstances. Perhaps you have taken early retirement or are about to move and want to take life at a more leisurely pace. Perhaps your change in

Is running a B&B the right thing for you to do?

- COPING WITH THE COMMITMENT AND THE CHANGE IN LIFESTYLE

- SOME QUESTIONS FOR YOU TO ASK YOURSELF

lifestyle has come about because your children have left home and you think their bedrooms could generate a little extra income. Or maybe you now work from home and you see the B&B as an effective use of your time and property. The idea may have been born out of necessity (for example, redundancy), or out of a change in family circumstances, which has required you to earn additional income while remaining at home. Alternatively, you may have stayed at a B&B and thought it seemed a pleasant way of earning a living, or that you could do it better.

Whatever the reason that has led you to this point, there are many things to think about before you go further. The idea of running a B&B can conjure up an image of being able to work from home while having lots of free time for yourself. After all, once breakfast has been cooked, the beds have been made and the guests have departed, there is really nothing else to do except wait for the next guests. If only that were true! Running a B&B represents not just a change of direction, but also a change in lifestyle.

SOME QUESTIONS FOR YOU TO ASK YOURSELF

Do you have what it takes, physically and mentally, to run a B&B? How will it affect your family and lifestyle? How would you feel about having strangers in your home? Have you thought through the financial implications?

Lets take each of these points in turn.

DO YOU HAVE WHAT IT TAKES?

The skills and qualities required for being a good host are numerous. Being positive, having patience, charm and humour, not being easily flustered and remaining calm at all times are some of the most important qualities to have, but it also helps if you are relatively fit and healthy. Life can become very busy even for the successful and for those who remain in control.

To help you consider this, let us look at what is involved in a typical day of someone running a B&B.

Case Study
What needs to be done in the typical day of a B&B?

*   Be up and ready in time to prepare and cook breakfasts – some guests may need to be up and out by half past seven, so you will need to be up by half past six.

*   Serve breakfast (often at different times), and take time to talk to your guests and ensure they have everything they need.

*   When guests have left the dining room, clear and tidy dishes and prepare bills for anyone departing.

*   After the guests have left for the day, start cleaning the bedrooms, bathrooms and public areas ready for new arrivals; make beds and tidy all areas for those guests staying on.

*   Do daily routines: laundry, shopping, ironing and any daily maintenance – wear and tear will be greater than in a domestic household, and paintwork may need touching up, light bulbs replacing, kettles de-scaling, the garden weeding and the grass cutting (these aspects are all important in ensuring a positive first impression).

*   Complete paperwork (you are running a business) pay invoices, send out brochures, and respond to any enquiries, by phone or e-mail.

*   Welcome your new guests when the ringing of the front doorbell announces their arrival.

*   Explain everything, before offering them a cup of tea and advice on where to go for dinner.

Is running a B&B the right thing for you to do?

- COPING WITH THE COMMITMENT AND THE CHANGE IN LIFESTYLE

- SOME QUESTIONS FOR YOU TO ASK YOURSELF

Not all days are quite so hectic as the day described in the case study. Days when you have no bookings may be quieter, and days when there is a local event or a wedding in the area may be busier. And, of course, the case study does not take into account the ongoing maintenance of your home, spring-cleaning or any unforeseen situations that require immediate attention. Remember, unless you employ staff, you will be the waiter, cleaner, cook, porter, gardener, book-keeper, decorator, administrator – so you can expect to work long hours.

HOW WILL A B&B AFFECT MY FAMILY AND LIFESTYLE?
Your B&B will be a business – what is often referred to in the tourism industry as a micro business – but it differs from nearly all other businesses in that it remains first and foremost your home. Many guests choose to stay in a B&B, as opposed to a hotel, because they want to experience a home-from-home environment. But you will need to manage how the guest fits in with your family and how your family fits around your guests. If you have children are they able to use the public areas that guests use, such as the sitting room? How will guests welcome young children, piles of homework and trainers in the hallway? After all, some guests may have come away to have a break from their own young children.

Consider also how running a B&B from your home may the affect your own family and social life. Will you have to refuse invitations because the guests who were due at six o'clock have still not arrived at nine o'clock? Is there anyone who can cover for you when you attend the school play or take the children to the dentist? Do you have contingency plans for the time you are ill and there are six guests booked in for that evening? Will your family react badly to losing their privacy?

HOW WOULD YOU FEEL ABOUT HAVING STRANGERS IN YOUR HOME?
There are important questions to ask yourself before you start to run a B&B. Do you really like people? It's an important question and requires a genuine answer. Dealing with people requires skill, tact and diplomacy. Are you flexible? You might immediately answer yes, but no two guests are the same. Even if, for every difficult guest you come across, you meet many absolutely straightforward and often fascinating individuals, you will need to be sure that you can deal with the difficult guest, too. Can you cope with the guest who constantly wants to ask you questions and does not seem to

want to leave? Or the guest who uses both twin beds over a two-night stay? Or those who do not arrive when they said they would and then claim they wanted a twin room, when you know they booked a double? Will you find it difficult not to clean up immediately you see that guests have left footprints in the entrance hall? Can you cope with 'unreasonable' requests, without letting guests know they are being difficult? Can you show tolerance to the awkward guest?

Case Study

B&B – An operator's view

There were only the two of us, and setting up a B&B in the early days was an idea that came about when my husband and I bought a new house that was the right price but larger than we had planned. Two things occurred to us: the house needed doing up, and it had the potential to earn money. Realising that potential was not going to let us get the best from the house for ourselves in the early days, so we had to have a long-term view. Our first priority was to make the twin bedroom, bathroom and dining room ready for guests. It meant that we had to sleep in a room that definitely was not the best in the house, and I remember it was rather a 'work-in-progress'! John was working full-time on split shifts and I left my hotel job when the rooms were completed. Because I had an idea of how the business worked, I got in touch with the tourist board and the local Tourist Information Centre (TIC) to publicise our business.

We opened in the spring, which, as it turned out, was a good time of year. I can remember being nervous about the first guest, a single lady auditor (who came back six months later!). She stayed for three nights, only had one (small) cooked breakfast and was very happy with the room.

My anxiety, if you can call it that, was that the guests should really like what we had done, and be comfortable – they did, and they still seem to.

continued

In the early days we got a grading of Listed, Highly Commended. Later, after we had added more plumbing and tweaked what we were offering (based on our own ideas and on our guests' feedback), we were able to get a four diamond grading.

I've been asked about high and low points. I do like (most of) the people, and the money that we have made has really kept the house going and helped to pay for a lot of the work that we've done. What I will say is that I really don't like having a week full of one-nighters. We have three rooms now and the slog of servicing them all each day can be very demanding. The other thing I'll mention is the phone. Not wanting to miss out on the bookings means you'll never escape the phone – you might take a booking in the supermarket car park (my phone is diverted to my mobile). But on balance it's all worth it, because we enjoy it.

WHAT ARE THE FINANCIAL IMPLICATIONS?

For most people developing a B&B there are important financial considerations. How much will it cost you? Will you make money? The costs can vary tremendously. At one end of the scale, all you may need to do is to make fine adjustments to your existing home: perhaps your children have left home or are going to university and you will be using their rooms. At the other end of the scale, you may be planning to relocate and buy a property specifically for use as a B&B, or you may be purchasing an existing operation. Apart from the costs of purchasing a property, there will be fees for estate agents, solicitors and surveyors long before you start to equip and furnish your B&B, and reap the dividends. You may be considering borrowing money, which in turn will require a business plan, an operating budget and cash flow forecast.

If your plans include taking a loan then it is worth approaching a bank: all banks can offer help for those wanting to start a business; most will be able to provide a 'Business start-up pack'.

Is your property right for use as a B&B?

Is your property right
for use as a B&B?
- LOCATION
- COST
- FACILITIES
- QUALITY
- WHO WILL STAY?

This section asks you to consider whether your property will work as a B&B. Will it provide the flexibility to accommodate both your guests and also your family? Does it offer enough space for everyone, allow easy access and provide parking? Is it suitably located?

To start answering these questions it is worth considering what makes guests choose a particular B&B. For many guests, a choice of B&B may be related to location. For others, the main consideration may be cost, and for others it may be the facilities. Most guests, however, arrive at the final decision on which B&B to stay at after considering all these factors, including the all-important consideration of quality (which will be discussed in more detail in later chapters).

LOCATION

Most guests choose a B&B for its location. They may be staying in or around your area for work, to attend an event or to visit friends and relatives. Guests on holiday or those who are taking a short break may have a wider choice of locations, and other considerations may have affected their final choice.

The problem is, what do you do if you are not in the right location? After all, you cannot move your property from what you feel to be a difficult location. The factors to consider here are: Will your location draw guests to you? What reasons will they have to be in your area? And what features or local places of interest may you want to use in promoting your location as the one to choose over others?

Take, as an example, a B&B which is a semi-detached property on the edge of a large town. It is not near the station and therefore does not easily attract guests arriving on public transport. It is on a busy road and therefore does not attract guests looking for a quiet weekend break. However, it is near the main roads and easily attracts business people and guests with their own transport who are attending functions or visiting family.

You can weigh up the pros and cons of any location and relate them to the type of guest you may attract. This is a useful exercise as it may help you decide how to equip and develop your B&B.

COST

Cost is usually a consideration for guests when they are deciding on a B&B. But guests are not just price-sensitive – they are also price-conscious. Being price-sensitive means that the cost becomes the most important factor in choosing the B&B. Price-sensitive guests usually select the cheapest option because they are on a very tight budget. But being price-conscious means that price becomes linked to quality, and other factors start to affect the decision. As a general principle, people tend to associate price with quality, although the association is never, of course, exact. Few guests, however, will opt for the cheapest B&B unless they have to, because they will think that there must be a catch or simply that the price signifies lower quality. Guests who are after high quality will be attracted to a higher-priced B&B, whereas other guests will opt for a mid-priced B&B because they feel happier with the level of quality that they associate with that price. Unless you specifically want to target the higher end of the market – where guests are willing to pay for a higher level of service and hospitality – you should therefore select a price that is neither too high nor too low.

FACILITIES

A wide range of facilities can be found in B&Bs throughout the country from basic accommodation to full leisure facilities. As living standards have improved, so too have guests' expectations. Some guests will be used to en-suite bathrooms in their own homes. Business travellers may be looking for rooms with good working space and convenient power for their laptops. Some guests may also want to be able to use the dining room in the evenings so that they can bring back a takeaway meal. Large grounds and gardens could be an added attraction for guests.

It is also essential at this stage to be aware of the Disability Discrimination Act (DDA). The DDA requires services to be accessible for all guests while considering what is reasonable for the business. For B&Bs, the implications of the Act will primarily be felt by disabled guests, but there are benefits for all guests and bringing your B&B in line with the DDA can help to increase the appeal your B&B. There is more information on the DDA in Chapter 3.

Is your property right for use as a B&B?
- LOCATION
- COST
- FACILITIES
- QUALITY
- WHO WILL STAY?

QUALITY

While all these aspects may influence the guests' choice of where to stay, guests are also concerned about the quality of the accommodation they are about to book. Booking accommodation is one of those purchases where you are buying something sight unseen. When buying accommodation, you are committing yourself to spending money, and yet you will not have tried the bed or experienced the breakfast. How do you know your purchase will match or even exceed your expectations?

The best form of advertising you will ever have is word of mouth. The customer chooses a B&B on the basis of a trusted recommendation. That gives them some reassurance of the level of quality they will experience; without word of mouth the guest has no indication of quality. The National Quality Assurance Schemes (NQAS) provide quality ratings that guests can use to make an informed and quality assured decision on where to stay. We will focus on the NQAS in Chapter 4.

WHO WILL STAY?

Not all tourists are holidaymakers, even though our impression of the tourist is often fixed on this image. When the tourist board uses the term 'tourists' it refers to anyone who is away from their home. And when you consider the separate reasons why people may be travelling away from home, the definition of a tourist becomes very broad indeed.

So among those people who are staying away from home, who is looking for a B&B to stay in? Broadly speaking guests fall into one of two categories: those who are away for leisure and those who are away for work. But within these two categories there are many reasons why people stay away from home. They may be visiting friends or family but are unable to stay with them, or they may be attending a wedding, party or other event. They may on holiday or having a long weekend away. Perhaps they are travelling on business, attending a conference, or on a training course. They may be working in the area, moving jobs and about to move home. People stay away for many different reasons and they have many different requirements when they do so. We look at the needs of different guests in Chapters 5, 6 and 7.

What are the costs?

Will your property need any alterations if it is to be run as a B&B? What are the costs of setting up the B&B? Even if you believe that your property is perfectly suitable without any major alterations, there may still be other costs to take into account.

These costs include insurance, advertising and promotion, planning permission and any professional charges. In addition, adapting your house to work as a B&B may involve:

- insulation and soundproofing
- upgrading the hot water boiler to a larger capacity
- increasing the number of electric sockets and getting all electrical equipment checked to meet safety regulations
- addition of an extractor fan in bathrooms
- redecoration, carpeting or re-flooring
- additional furniture for bedrooms, the dining room and any other areas
- extra towelling
- bedding, table linen, crockery, cutlery, locks and keys
- accessories, such as kettles, hairdryers, TVs and radios in the bedrooms
- toiletries in the bathroom.

And of course, it is not just the areas the guest uses that will need attention. You may need larger or additional kitchen equipment, such as a toaster, additional pans, a second kettle, a coffee maker, a larger washing machine and tumble dryer, and a professional iron or ironing machine if you plan to do your own laundry. You may feel you need a powerful vacuum cleaner and perhaps even an additional fridge. As you can see, there are a lot of considerations.

Are you ready?

Deciding to start a B&B can mean a change in routine and lifestyle, may affect others, and can be very hard work. The income may be variable, the hours are unpredictable, it can be hard work, and it may affect your social life. However, as any owner will tell you, running a B&B can also be extremely rewarding. You get the opportunity to be your own boss, to have control of your own business, to take holidays when you want, meet a wide variety of people, and incur no travel costs 'going to work'. You can also make a comfortable living. All in all, there are far more advantages than disadvantages.

Whether you have a new property, are using your existing home or have bought an existing B&B, you will need to know how to set up a B&B from scratch. Chapter 2 looks at planning your business from Day One. It offers helpful advice on some of the most important legal issues and on the research you should undertake to understand your location and the nature of tourism in your area.

What are the costs?

Are you ready?

Chapter 2
Planning

This chapter looks at research you can carry out to assess the strengths of your area, compare different types of visitor and their specific needs, and consider some legal issues before getting started.

Whether your plan is to purchase a property or to develop your existing home into a business, you will need to consider the appropriateness of the location. Wherever you choose, it's advisable to carry out considerable research to see whether it's a viable location in which to set up.

The location of the B&B will, to a degree, determine your market. Why do guests come to the area? Are they seasonal visitors or year-round visitors? Are there many other B&Bs nearby, and are they busy?

Your location

It has been said before, but the three key aspects of a successful business are location, location and location. This is as true of B&Bs as it is of any other business. Many B&B owners will, of course tell you that their location is the right location, but, as we saw in Chapter 1, wherever you are located there is likely to be a market for you: a quiet rural location may appeal to couples looking for peace and quiet; a busy city-centre location may be perfect for a businessperson attending a meeting the next day; proximity to universities,

conference centres, large hotels and airports all offer
potential for business. The challenge is to recognise these
markets and ensure that what you offer meets the needs of
your prospective guests.

Your location

– CITY AND TOWNS

– COUNTRYSIDE

– SEASIDE

– OTHER
CONSIDERATIONS

CITY AND TOWNS

The benefits of a town or city location are that you are likely
to be closer to major road networks and rail and bus stations,
so that it will be easier for guests to reach your property.
A nearby airport or ferry terminal can lead to visitors staying
overnight, and places of work – such as industrial units,
factories, head offices or training centres – can draw people
into an area. And, if a town or city has colleges, universities
and hospitals, people will want somewhere to stay when they
are visiting friends or family.

Generally, there will be more passing trade in cities and in
towns than there is in other locations. However, as in any
busy environment, there is also likely to be more competition,
stronger pressure to keep prices low and greater variance in
the booking pattern – for example, more guests are likely to
stay for one night only.

COUNTRYSIDE

The benefits of a countryside location are various. A tranquil
environment can prove attractive to guests wanting peace
and quiet. Nearby national parks, visitor attractions (such
as historic houses and gardens) or coastal scenery may all
encourage leisure guests. Country house hotels holding
weddings and functions often produce a demand for
accommodation: wedding guests may not want to stay in the
hotel or may find the hotel's rates too expensive, and B&B
accommodation may prove more attractive. If you are in an
area suitable for walking, bird watching or other specialist
activity, you may find a healthy demand for accommodation.
A positive difference from towns and cities is that visitors
to the countryside are often likely to stay for more than one
night. The bad news is that there is usually less chance to
pick up passing or same-day trade and you may need to work
harder to promote your property. There may also be less
demand for accommodation all year round. You may find
the winter months (the 'off-season') very quiet, autumn

and spring (the 'shoulder season') unpredictable and the summer (the 'high season') so busy that you will be turning guests away.

SEASIDE

Seaside accommodation brings many benefits. A lot of families want to take a traditional seaside holiday and will stay for a long weekend or up to seven nights, drawn by the entertainment offered in the area. Coastal resorts will also often host conventions or trade exhibitions, which bring in lots of visitors and exhibitors. Seasonality could affect your business; as with countryside accommodation, you may find the off-season and shoulder months much quieter. But, come high season, you might have such demand that you need to manage your bookings carefully to make the most of your lettings, and may therefore avoid one-nighters, especially in the middle of the week. As with town and city locations, there will be a lot of competition, which may keep prices down.

OTHER CONSIDERATIONS

If you live in a residential area and plan to convert your own property to a B&B, it is worth considering your neighbours. Ask yourself whether you would welcome it if they decided to open a B&B. If you live in a rural or peaceful area, your neighbours may be concerned about extra noise, vehicles coming and going and parking arrangements. It is often a good idea to talk to your neighbours first, explaining what you are planning to do and reassuring them that there will be no disruption to the neighbourhood.

Who will be your guests?

BUSINESS TRAVELLERS

In city and urban areas, you are often likely to attract business travellers, which will almost inevitably mean single occupancy. Business travellers may be attending a meeting, on a training course or at a conference. They may be working in the area for just one night or could be frequent visitors to the area as part of a long-term project. They may be the person in charge of a building project, the regional manager of a supermarket group or someone working in a new job before moving to the area.

Business travellers may stay for more than one night; indeed, if they are working on a long-term project, or their house move takes longer than expected, they might want accommodation for a few nights every week for many months. They will often have specific needs and requirements, such as safe and secure off-road parking, and an early breakfast; some, particularly female business travellers, will want an evening meal. Against that, however, most business travellers will usually be away for the remainder of the day.

CONTRACTORS

Wherever there are building works – whether of new homes or a new factory or road – there will be a demand for B&B accommodation. Depending on the work being done, contractors may need to stay for many weeks or months. They may be working long hours, will usually want an early breakfast and may need additional space to park their vans.

SCHOOLS, COLLEGES AND UNIVERSITIES

If you are located in a university town or a town with a public school, students will need places for their families to stay when visiting. The demand for accommodation is particularly high at the start and end of terms and at graduations (typically in October or July). Foreign language schools and universities with a high proportion of foreign students can generate demand for accommodation for families visiting from overseas. Visiting lecturers and professors often need places to stay and will have particular needs – they may want to work in the evenings and will require generous and level workspace, power points, even internet and e-mail access.

OTHER VISITORS

Many other types of visitors require accommodation – actors performing in a local theatre, traders attending a craft show or antiques fair, participants in sports events and demonstrators working at local events.

Your location
- CITY AND TOWNS
- COUNTRYSIDE
- SEASIDE
- OTHER
  CONSIDERATIONS

Who will be your guests?
- BUSINESS
  TRAVELLERS
- CONTRACTORS
- SCHOOLS, COLLEGES
  AND UNIVERSITIES
- OTHER VISITORS
- LEISURE GUESTS
- THE FAMILY MARKET
- KNOW THE TRENDS
- YOUR COMPETITORS

LEISURE GUESTS

Leisure guests will stay for many different reasons. Whether they have come to visit an historic town, to take advantage of a city break or to enjoy a peaceful environment, they are likely to want to relax; they will not want to feel under pressure to leave after breakfast, and they may well want to be able to come back early in the afternoon. Alternatively, if they have come to attend an event, concert or show, they may well want to be able to return at a much later hour than normal.

Walkers and cyclists also come in the category of leisure guests, as do other guests engaging in specialist activities. Walkers and cyclists will have specific needs, such as somewhere to dry clothes, to store bikes safely and a place to leave muddy boots. Their needs will be very different from those of the leisurely visitor: they may require early breakfasts and packed lunches, and they may be back early to relax before dinner.

Wedding guests may arrive, wanting to get changed, long before the time that you would normally welcome guests and may then not return until the early hours. Other leisure guests may be visiting friends or relatives who are unable to accommodate them, or attending a christening or a funeral.

THE FAMILY MARKET

Families with young children may want family rooms, with cots or bunk beds for the children. They may need highchairs at breakfast and plenty of storage space in the bedroom. They may also want their hosts to provide toys and games if the weather is not so good. Typically, seaside visitors can often book far in advance and may often want a longer stay. A reason for this type of business may be the presence of a single grandparent in the party, and you may find that there is more demand for a single room with a high-backed chair than you had expected.

KNOW THE TRENDS

There are distinct trends in the letting year, and in Chapter 8 we will look at how to grow your business and how to identify the peaks and troughs. At this stage, you need merely to be aware that, for most B&B owners, there will be peak months – when there may be a lack of accommodation in the area and it becomes a sellers' market – and very slow periods, when the telephone never rings and the rooms are always empty.

It is an oversimplification, but a typical year for many B&B owners will be a relatively quiet winter with a busy summer. Within the year there will, however, always be opportunities to pick up business, in the form of an annual air show, a firework display, a regatta or a rally, an outdoor concert or a festival. A useful idea is to map out the year by identifying events in each month. This can be a very useful way of predicting when you should be busy, and it also provides useful information when it comes to knowing how to let your rooms: should you take a booking for just one night, when you know there is a classical music festival lasting three days?

YOUR COMPETITORS

At first, you may think that the other B&Bs in your area are competitors. After all, you are all competing for the same market. But consider this again. If a nearby B&B is full and receives an enquiry, either by telephone, or from their local Tourist Information Centre, then whom can they pass the business on to? If you have a good relationship with your neighbouring B&Bs, you may quickly reap the benefits of referral business.

Researching the competition will help highlight how busy the area is, the level of quality being offered and the rates other B&Bs are charging. Here are some suggestions for how you should go about your research.

STEP 1 – INFORMATION FROM OTHER OPERATORS

A good first step for anyone considering opening a B&B is to research the competition by obtaining their brochures and tariff charges. Part of this can be done by using the internet (and the VisitBritain website) or by means of local accommodation guides that cover the area. You will still have only an approximate idea of tariffs and it is worth ringing various establishments to find out what is included. Different tariffs may reflect different extras such as en-suite rooms,

Who will be your guests?

- BUSINESS TRAVELLERS
- CONTRACTORS
- SCHOOLS, COLLEGES AND UNIVERSITIES
- OTHER VISITORS
- LEISURE GUESTS
- THE FAMILY MARKET
- KNOW THE TRENDS
- YOUR COMPETITORS

very high quality standards or additional facilities, such as a swimming pool, tennis court or Jacuzzi.

It important to make your enquiry by telephone, because the rates advertised by other B&Bs are often only a guide. If you are uncomfortable about this, say you will be needing somewhere for your family to stay when they are visiting you.

STEP 2 – CONTACT YOUR TOURIST INFORMATION CENTRE

To get the best idea of the tariffs in your area and for an objective point of view, contact your local Tourist Information Centre (TIC), or Visitor Information Centre, for help and advice. TIC staff deal will deal with up to a thousand enquiries a day from people walking in or telephoning, receive e-mails and distribute tens of thousands of accommodation guides. In addition, thousands of people visit their website daily to find accommodation. Because they make bookings on a daily basis, the staff can provide you with excellent advice on how busy an area is, as well as on the peaks and troughs in the year, and the events that can generate high demand for accommodation. The TIC may also be able to provide information on any future local developments (such as business parks or new houses projects) that may bring in additional demand for accommodation.

If you are uncertain about how many rooms to let or what to charge, the TIC will also be able to provide you with a local accommodation guide, which will help you start to think about both issues. This guide will be a useful place to start your research. It will contain a list of the B&Bs in your area – often with details of the number of bedrooms, their tariff and their location. This information will help you work out how you may fit into the overall picture, and will give you an idea of what you will be able to charge for accommodation.

STEP 3 – CONTACT OTHER B&BS

It is also worth approaching a B&B operator away from the area in which you plan to set up and talk to them. Many will be very proud of what they do and will be happy to show you around and discuss the 'highs and lows'.

Perhaps most importantly, consider joining a local B&B group; groups are a helpful resource for comparing notes, learning from other operators who may be much more experienced than yourself, and for sharing business. There are many national and local groups throughout the country.

Case Study
Working together – an example of an accommodation group

The Bedfordshire & Hertfordshire Farm & Country Accommodation Group is a good example of an industry grouping that acts as a kind of co-operative. It does not set out to have fiercely commercial aims for itself, but to provide a support mechanism for its members. It started some 21 years ago with three members and now has about 25 small operators, covering mainly B&Bs but also some self-catering operations. It uses subscriptions from its membership to add strength to its limited marketing activity. This has included the production of a group brochure promoted through the member organisations, local TICs and businesses, and at leaflet swap-shops in conjunction with visitor attractions and various shows and events. Enterprisingly, its latest venture is to redesign the group website, which has been recognised as an increasingly important portal for enquiries and bookings. A new feature will be to create more hyperlinks, into and out of the site, which are particularly useful for potential customers visiting the website of a nearby attraction for information on a weekend event.

The greatest advantage of the group, however, is the referral aspect that it brings. Small B&B operators in a busy area with a lot of business tourism can often become full, and it is an extended service to the customer, and to each other, to refer bookings on to another group member (all the group members are quality assured). All group members know each other, or know of each other, very well partly as the result of a modest but vibrant social programme, which also helps to provide cohesiveness.

How much do I charge?

The prices charged by B&Bs vary considerably throughout the country. Some B&Bs in more-sensitive local markets attempt to encourage guests by keeping their prices very low. B&Bs in other areas charge a price similar to that of hotels, as a reflection of a higher quality. Setting the right price for your B&B is a challenging task. For a start, the industry prices itself very differently from other industries. When you are buying a product such as a camera or a car, the price charged will at least in part be related to the cost of manufacturing the product. With a B&B many of the costs you incur would have been incurred in any case by you and your family: the cost of heating and lighting the house, or looking after the garden, are costs that any domestic home would have to face, and it may be difficult to determine the actual cost of operating the B&B, especially before you have even started.

WHAT WILL IT COST?

The operating costs and overheads you will incur will include heating and light, wear and tear to carpets and decoration (both of which may need attending to more regularly than you might normally), staff salaries, higher costs of laundry and food, advertising charges, and any interest and loan repayments. As a starting point, it will be useful to work out your current household expenses and the annual cost of all your utilities. You can then compare your actual costs at the end of the first year with your estimate of the domestic costs of your property, and this process will give you some indication of some of the annual costs of running your B&B.

This process will also reveal some 'hidden' costs to running a B&B. These may include upgrading your domestic washing machine, buying a larger fridge and a separate freezer – possibly buying a tumble-dryer if you feel that hanging the washing out every day is going to be impractical. Think carefully before you buy any goods of this kind, because careful planning and management will reduce the costs of running a B&B. For example, selecting more energy-efficient products – such as condenser boilers, low-energy light bulbs and dual-flush toilets – can help you save on your operating costs. (We will look in more detail at equipping the B&B in Chapter 4.)

How much do I charge?

- WHAT WILL IT COST?

- SETTING YOUR RATES

SETTING YOUR RATES

Obviously, you need to set your rates to cover your costs, but what should you charge on top of that? Or maybe a more appropriate question would be what could you charge?

Think about the competition in your area. By now you will have done some research and will know how much others are charging for a single room, or single occupancy, and how much they charge for a double. In addition, you will have seen what facilities they provide – for example, whether the bathroom is en suite. If the B&B is graded, you will have noted its quality rating, and you may have established that the higher the quality rating the more the B&B charges (though this is not always the case). That said, some operators who achieve a higher rating are content to use the pulling power of the higher rating while keeping their prices very competitive.

There may be instances where you want to charge a rate that reflects the exceptional quality of what you are offering – or your B&B may be in a 'honey pot' location, which allows you to aim for a higher rate. This may be a sound decision based on an accurate understanding of your business, but you should be aware that it is likely to put you into a very different price category from that of other B&Bs in your area. Generally speaking, it is a good idea to make sure that your rates are not vastly different from those of the competition – it is going to be the local market, your competitors and their rates that ultimately determine how much you can charge.

Think carefully about your own facilities before you set your rate, and take what other B&Bs are offering into account. You need to be able to make a fair comparison between the amenities they offer and those that you can offer. Do other B&Bs accept pets, provide off-road parking, a lounge, family rooms or gardens?

As well as setting rates relative to other B&Bs, you may also charge different rates for each room. You may not be able to charge as much for rooms with a shared bathroom as for those with en suite facilities; standard bed sizes may not command as high a rate as king-size beds, and an en suite bathroom with a separate shower may have more appeal and command a higher rate than a shower room.

Once you have decided on your rates, think about how to advertise them. Consider a single-room rate and a double-room rate, rather than a rate per person. Always include breakfast in the rate and bear in mind that the majority of guests will expect the option of a full cooked breakfast, even if they do not take it up – so, if you decide not to provide a full cooked breakfast, and choose to offer only continental, you must make sure that you advertise this clearly, and that you mention it on booking.

Apart from the standard rates, you may also need to consider whether you intend to have any other rates. Some proprietors charge a single-room rate that is only a little less than the double rate, on the basis that the laundry costs and cleaning will be much the same for one guest as they are for two. And what about a reduced rate for children? You may have decided not to take children but, if you do, will you offer a reduced rate for a young child? A child will almost always sleep in a family room and, while there will be some additional laundry costs, the child will probably eat less breakfast. And have you considered a discounted rate for longer stays, a midweek and weekend rate, or an off-season rate? It is common practice to offer a discounted rate for guests who stay for three nights or more, as the laundry and servicing costs are reduced, but it is useful to contact other B&B owners to see how they charge – and then to mirror their practices.

How to manage your lettings

Many B&Bs operate a policy of not taking a one-night stay at the weekend or midweek in order to make the most of their bookings. Take, for example, a three-day event in your area, starting on Thursday and ending late Saturday. This gives you the chance to take bookings for three, or even four nights, and many guests may be looking for a minimum three-night stay. But, if you have let a room on the Friday for just one night, you may not be able to let that room for the other nights, and you could lose out.

Identifying periods of high demand will help you manage your bookings. Ask your Tourist Information Centre (you should by now have made contact with them) what the peak periods are, mark these in your letting diary, and manage your bookings accordingly.

How will you use your property?

Chapter 5 presents detailed advice on how to set up your B&B to meet the needs of your guests, but this section provides some suggestions for making good use of the space at your disposal.

When deciding on the number of rooms and the number of bed spaces that you want to let, you will need to consider carefully what space the guest will have once the room is furnished and equipped. Visitors stay in B&Bs, as opposed to hotels, because B&Bs offer a personal touch and homely environment – but guests also want and expect comfort and quality, which means ample space in the bedrooms and in the bathrooms. There is no comfort if a guest has to move a chair so that they can open the wardrobe door, or crane their necks to watch TV because it is fixed to a wall and can only be viewed when the guest is sitting on the bed. One of the things guests find most annoying is when they have to squeeze into a tiny shower room, built in the corner of the bedroom, where there is no space for their wash bag and little space to towel down.

You will need to cater for the fact that guests' expectations from B&Bs are much higher than they were 12 to 15 years ago. This is where you could make expensive mistakes if you do not plan carefully. Whether you are building from new, adapting an existing B&B, or converting your home, consider making scale drawings of your rooms. These drawings should take into account all the electrical points that will be required, as well as any plumbing that will need to be installed. Once you have done that, position all the furnishings (again to scale) you plan to have for each room. This will enable you to decide whether the available space means that it is possible to fit in twin beds, as opposed to a double bed, or whether you are trying to overfill a small room that is really suited as a single. There is growing demand for single accommodation, even though many B&B single rooms have very limited space.

If you are thinking of attracting the family market, you will need to be able to add a single bed to the bedroom. But this room may also be sold to couples, and you should take into account that the additional single bed may restrict their level of comfort. Consider the flexibility of the room – is it worth investing in zip-and-link beds? These can either provide twin beds or a large double, when they are zipped together.

Designing the room layout is easier if you are starting from scratch; if you are using existing fixtures, there will be other points to consider. If you are you replacing all the furniture, or just some of it, you will need to have an idea of the style of the room that you want to create. Base this on the type of guest you hope to attract. Are you hoping for couples wanting to be pampered, for whom the dressed four-poster bed will be a wow, or for the business traveller, who will need a good desk area, possibly extra power points, and a comfortable chair?

If your family are still living at home, think carefully about how their rooms work in relation to the guests' rooms. Would it make sense to swap rooms around so that the family is all at one end of the house and the paying guests at the other, possibly with the quieter rooms or with a better view? The rooms you select for guests may also depend upon the bathroom arrangements. It is still perfectly acceptable for guests to share a bathroom, but there is a growing expectation to have an en suite or private bathroom.

Do not be tempted to use rooms that are used by members of the family who go away for the weekend. A visitor who is paying money to stay with you will not appreciate opening a chest of drawers or a wardrobe and finding personal belongings and clothing.

There are legal issues you need to be aware of, even if you are setting up a B&B from home, without any changes to the property. The next chapter reviews some of the legal considerations you need to be aware of, and outlines some of the principal laws and regulations that affect the operation of a B&B.

Chapter 3

Legal considerations

If you are thinking about running a B&B, you will need to be aware of your legal position. This chapter takes a look at the areas of legislation that are likely to be of most concern to you. These are:

- planning consent
- building regulations
- business rates
- fire safety

This chapter does not contain definitive legal advice, and is designed merely to make you aware of the key issues that need to be considered. For more-detailed advice on legal considerations for B&Bs, please consult the Pink Booklet, from which the information in this chapter has been adapted. This guide to legislation and other regulations affecting accommodation businesses is available from VisitBritain (contact details are in Chapter 10).

Essential first steps

You may already have an idea about what kind of guest your B&B is likely to attract, and you may want to tailor your property to meet their needs. Before you start knocking down walls and buying beds and accessories, however, you will need to make sure that you have met the legal requirements for running a B&B.

The first thing you need to do if you are thinking about running a B&B is to get planning permission (and building regulations, where applicable). If you are considering starting a new business, or converting or extending your premises, contact the planning department of your local authority at a very early stage, and possibly their tourism officer, for their advice on planning permission.

Any structural alterations to a property, or the construction of a new building, will be subject to building regulations. But you may also need 'change of use' planning permission even if your ambitions are more modest, for example if you are simply thinking of offering bed and breakfast in your home, or equipping an existing building without carrying out any structural alterations to the property.

The policies on granting planning permission vary from one local authority to another. Among the issues that an authority may take into consideration when deciding whether planning permission is necessary, or when considering an application, are the effects on neighbours, car-parking facilities and the number of bedrooms offered for letting. You may also need consent for any signage for your property.

BUSINESS RATE

You will need to pay business rates if you are running a B&B and do not fall within any of the categories below.

(a) You do not intend to offer short-stay accommodation to more than six people at any one time.
(b) You, the owner, occupy part of the property as your only or main home.
(c) Your house is primarily for use as your home and only secondarily for letting out the rooms (for this you will need to consider the length of your season, the scale of modifications undertaken for guests, and the proportion of the house you occupy).

If you have to pay business rates, but use your property for business and domestic purposes, it is only the part of the property that you use for business purposes that is subject to business rates; the domestic accommodation is liable to Council Tax. Where parts of a house have a shared use – for example, a kitchen or dining room – a decision will be made by the valuation officer on whether a particular room is included as business or domestic property. No room or part of the property will be counted twice.

HOW ARE BUSINESS RATES CALCULATED?

If you need to pay business rates, your property will have a 'Rateable Value' based on the rental value of your property – this value will be set by an independent government agency, the Valuation Office Agency (VOA).

Your local authority will calculate your business rates by multiplying the Rateable Value of your property by a multiplier or 'poundage' set each year by the government.

You can obtain details of the Rateable Value of your property from your local valuation office or the business rates department of your local authority. Entries in local rating lists can be found on the VOA website: www.voa.gov.uk.

If your assessment shows that you are liable for business rates, this will affect your outgoings and profitability, depending on occupancy, as it represents a fixed cost. You can lodge an appeal against a valuation (the VOA can advise you how to do this), but this can be a lengthy process.

Fire safety in accommodation

B&Bs that come within the scope of the Fire Precautions (Hotels and Boarding Houses) Order 1972 must comply with the fire certification requirements of the Fire Precautions Act 1971.

FIRE CERTIFICATES – WHO NEEDS THEM?

Fire certificates are issued by your local fire authority, and describe the fire safety arrangements for your property (including emergency routes and exits, fire fighting equipment and warning procedures).

If you are converting your property for use as a B&B, you are advised to contact your local fire authority as early as possible to see whether you need a fire certificate.

You will need a fire certificate if your B&B provides sleeping accommodation for more than six people (whether guests or staff), excluding permanent resident members of the family; and you will also need one if you provide any sleeping accommodation (whether for guests or staff) above the first floor or below the ground floor of your establishment. However, if the sleeping accommodation you provide is for no more than six people (guests and staff) and is on the first and/or ground floor only, you will not need a fire certificate.

If you need a fire certificate, it is an offence to use premises without one, unless your application is pending (see below).

If you are in any doubt as to whether or not you need a fire certificate, you are strongly advised to seek the opinion of your local fire authority.

FREQUENTLY ASKED QUESTIONS

(a)   Do my family or I count as staff?

The owner and his or her family are not usually included in the six-person limit. Likewise, fire officers would not include areas in the property that are for the owner's own domestic use as 'sleeping accommodation for staff'.

(b)   What happens if I have more than six bed spaces, but never take more than six guests at one time?

The 1972 Order talks of the 'provision' of sleeping accommodation for more than six persons. According to the Home Office, which implements the 1971 Act, this refers to the number of available bed spaces. In other words, if you have seven bed spaces, you must have a fire certificate.

The word 'provision' has, however, proved to be open to a range of different interpretations. Some local fire authorities may not require a fire certificate for smaller establishments that undertake not to accommodate more than six persons at one time, even though there are more than six bed spaces available. If this is your position, you should get written confirmation from your local fire authority in case of any later issue concerning your fire safety arrangements. (Remember that fire certificates are always required if there is any guest accommodation above the first floor or below the ground floor.)

Essential first steps
- BUSINESS RATE
- HOW ARE BUSINESS RATES CALCULATED?

Fire safety in accommodation
- FIRE CERTIFICATES – WHO NEEDS THEM?
- RESPONSIBILITY FOR FIRE PRECAUTIONS
- B&B ACCOMMODATION
- FIRE SAFETY IN THE WORKPLACE

A definitive interpretation of 'provision' will be possible only if a test case is brought before the courts.

APPLYING FOR A FIRE CERTIFICATE

You must apply for a fire certificate through your local fire authority. They will be able to give you detailed advice on the precautions and procedures.

RESPONSIBILITY FOR FIRE PRECAUTIONS

The primary responsibility for fire precautions lies with the occupier of the premises.

Public liability insurance in relation to fire regulations/fire insurance

Before you start offering any form of accommodation, it is a good idea to contact your insurers.

If you provide accommodation for more than six people at any one time, and have not received or applied for a fire certificate, then any public liability insurance that you have may become void in the event of a guest being injured by fire. In such circumstances, you may become liable for unlimited damages. (And you should bear in mind that insurance companies apply a very strict definition of 'six bed spaces'.)

At the time of print, if you provide accommodation for more than six people and wish to participate in VisitBritain's National Quality Assurance Schemes, you must demonstrate to the assessor that either you have a fire certificate or you have applied for a fire certificate or you have written evidence from the local fire authority to show that a certificate is not required. For further information visit odpm.gov.uk

If you apply for your establishment to participate in the National Quality Assurance Schemes, you will have signed a code of conduct that includes your agreement to meet all your statutory obligations (including the Fire Precautions Act 1971).

For detailed advice on fire certificates and precautions, contact the local fire authority for the area in which your property is situated.

B&B ACCOMMODATION

The Fire Precautions Act 1971 does not identify any special precautions for premises that do not require a fire certificate, although it is clearly in everyone's interests that all establishments that offer accommodation are protected against the risk of fire.

However, even if your premises do not need to have a fire certificate, a fire authority still has the power to prohibit or restrict the use of your premises as sleeping accommodation if, in its opinion, there is a serious risk to life.

The building control department of your local authority may also specify certain fire safety measures if you are changing your property from 'private, domestic use' to 'providing serviced accommodation'.

FIRE SAFETY IN THE WORKPLACE

There are also regulations in place – the Fire Precautions (Workplace) Regulations 1997, as amended in 1999 – that make employers ultimately responsible for the safety of their employees in cases of fire in workplaces over which they have control. Under the regulations, employers are required to carry out fire-risk assessments on those workplaces (even if these include premises that are already covered by a fire certificate).

These regulations apply to you if you have one or more employees (and a part-time cleaner will count as an employee) working on your premises.

WHAT DO YOU NEED TO DO?

(a) Make an assessment. If you want to identify the precautions that you need to take to make sure the workplace complies with the Regulations, you need to make an assessment of the fire risks. The Regulations require appropriate:

*   fire-fighting equipment, fire detectors and alarms
*   fire-fighting measures and contacts with emergency service
*   emergency routes and exits
*   maintenance and repair of equipment.

Fire safety in accommodation

- FIRE CERTIFICATES –
  WHO NEEDS THEM?

- RESPONSIBILITY FOR
  FIRE PRECAUTIONS

- B&B
  ACCOMMODATION

- FIRE SAFETY IN
  THE WORKPLACE

What is appropriate will be determined by the size and layout of your premises, your activities, and the number of people who are working there.

You may already have carried out this risk assessment as part of a wider risk assessment, perhaps as part of your responsibilities under the Management of Health and Safety at Work Regulations 1999 (fire safety is part of the general safety issues covered by these regulations). Having a fire certificate will help enormously, as this will detail all your existing precautions, but it is not a substitute for doing the assessment.

(b) Keep a record. The regulations require employers of five or more people to keep a record of the assessment, and to have this available for inspection by the local fire authority, but even employers of fewer than five people should consider doing this, in case of any later issues concerning fire safety.

(c) Review. You are required to keep the assessment under review.

It is a criminal offence not to comply with the regulations, which it is the local fire authority's responsibility to enforce. Contact your local fire authority if you need advice on your risk assessment and the precautions you should take.

Other regulations that could affect you

The size and nature of your business will determine what you are required by law to do (and the Pink Booklet provides details on most of these requirements), but the other areas of legislation that you will need to be aware of in any case relate to:

- public liability insurance
- the Disability Discrimination Act (DDA)
- health and safety
- food safety
- TV licences
- the Trade Descriptions Act
- a register of your guests.

CAN I TURN GUESTS AWAY?

In most, but not all, instances the law will regard small B&Bs as 'private hotels'. As the owner of a private hotel you are free to pick and choose your guests even when rooms are available, provided that in exercising this right you are not discriminating on the grounds of disability, gender or race.

You cannot, however, turn away a guest who has made a prior booking, unless there are legal grounds for doing so. Such grounds might be that you had accepted the booking on the basis of statements, made by the guest, which turn out to be untrue. If, for example, you run a non-smoking B&B, you would be within your rights to turn away a couple who had said at the time of making the booking that they were non-smokers, but who start smoking on arrival – and you might also be able to claim damages from them.

THE DISABILITY DISCRIMINATION ACT

The Disability Discrimination Act (DDA) was introduced in 1995 to give disabled people new rights of access to goods, facilities and services – including accommodation. These rights are enforceable by any disabled individual through the courts, if necessary.

DOES THE ACT APPLY TO ME?

Yes. If you provide any sort of accommodation, the Act applies to you.

HOW DOES THE ACT DEFINE 'DISABLED'?

Disabled people are all those whose physical and mental impairments have a substantial and long-term adverse effect on their ability to carry out normal, day-to-day activities. The term includes those who have progressive conditions such as cancer, HIV, multiple sclerosis and muscular dystrophy, and who are likely to become increasingly disabled by their illness over time. These people become covered by the Act when their condition causes a noticeable effect on their ability to undertake day-to-day activities.

Fire safety in accommodation

- FIRE CERTIFICATES – WHO NEEDS THEM?

- RESPONSIBILITY FOR FIRE PRECAUTIONS

- B&B ACCOMMODATION

- FIRE SAFETY IN THE WORKPLACE

Other regulations that could affect you

- CAN I TURN GUESTS AWAY?

- THE DISABILITY DISCRIMINATION ACT

- TWO OTHER ACTS CONCERNING DISCRIMINATION

- OCCUPIERS' LIABILITY ACTS 1957 AND 1984

- HEALTH AND SAFETY AT WORK ACT 1974

- FOOD SAFETY ACT 1990

- FOOD SAFETY (GENERAL FOOD HYGIENE) REGULATIONS 1995

- TELEVISION LICENCES

- TRADE DESCRIPTIONS ACT 1968

- IMMIGRATION (HOTEL RECORDS) ORDER 1972 (AS AMENDED) – KEEPING A REGISTER OF YOUR GUESTS

The two most relevant parts of the Act relate to employment and access to goods, facilities and services. Your responsibilities with regard to guests are set out below.

As a 'service provider', you need to make sure that you treat disabled guests as you treat other guests, unless there is adequate justification for **less-favourable treatment**, such as health and safety regulations. You will be treating disabled guests less favourably if you refuse to serve them, offer them less favourable terms, or offer a lower standard of service compared with what you normally offer. Someone who is treated less favourably than others may, under the Act, seek damages from you through the county court.

You are also required to make **reasonable adjustments** to the way you deliver your services to make it easier for disabled guests to use them. If, for example, it is impossible or unreasonably difficult for a disabled person to use one of your services, you may need to change the relevant underlying practice, policy or procedure to make it easier; alternatively, you may need to provide another means of using your services (this does not require you to change your premises physically; that is covered below). Before you make any changes, it is advisable to check with a disabled person or disability organisation that your adjustments are appropriate (although you need to bear in mind that each disabled person is different and has different requirements).

Further examples of reasonable adjustments include: allowing blind people to bring their guide dogs, even if you do not normally allow guests to bring their pets to your premises; providing large-print menus for visually impaired guests; allowing disabled people to use a fully accessible side entrance to your B&B (with clear signage) when the front entrance has steps.

You are only required to do what is 'reasonable'. The resources at your disposal, and the cost and practicality of making your services accessible, will all have a bearing on what it is considered reasonable for you to do to make your services accessible to disabled people. What might be considered reasonable for a national hotel chain may not be so for a small B&B.

You have a duty as a service provider to take reasonable steps to remove, alter or prevent any physical barriers that make it impossible or unreasonably difficult for disabled people to make full use of your facilities, if the service cannot be provided by an alternative method. For the same reason, if you are planning building work or refurbishment, you should include disability-related changes at the same time. The planning or building department of your local authority will give you advice in this area, if you contact them before carrying out any such work.

Again, you are required to do only what is reasonable. For example, if you offer bed and breakfast with only two upstairs bedrooms, it would be unreasonable for you to carry out extensive and expensive building work to provide wheelchair access to these rooms.

Often, simple measures can make your facilities more accessible – for example, taking more time to help disabled guests, letting them know how to ask for help, and arranging appropriate training for you and your staff.

GOOD PRACTICE

There is a Code of Practice to help you comply with the terms and the spirit of the Act. In terms of what you should do in relation to disabled guests, this good practice includes:

- thinking and planning ahead
- not making assumptions based on stereotypes
- asking a disabled person or organisation, if you are in any doubt as to what to do
- respecting the dignity of your disabled guest
- establishing a positive policy and practices
- training staff, and yourself, accordingly.

TWO OTHER ACTS CONCERNING DISCRIMINATION

THE SEX DISCRIMINATION ACT 1975

This Act makes it unlawful to treat a person less favourably on the grounds of their sex. 'Less-favourable treatment on

---

Other regulations that could affect you

- CAN I TURN GUESTS AWAY?
- THE DISABILITY DISCRIMINATION ACT
- TWO OTHER ACTS CONCERNING DISCRIMINATION
- OCCUPIERS' LIABILITY ACTS 1957 AND 1984
- HEALTH AND SAFETY AT WORK ACT 1974
- FOOD SAFETY ACT 1990
- FOOD SAFETY (GENERAL FOOD HYGIENE) REGULATIONS 1995
- TELEVISION LICENCES
- TRADE DESCRIPTIONS ACT 1968
- IMMIGRATION (HOTEL RECORDS) ORDER 1972 (AS AMENDED) – KEEPING A REGISTER OF YOUR GUESTS

the grounds of sex' would include refusing a person a room because of their sex, or providing accommodation or services on less-favourable terms.

THE RACE RELATIONS ACT *1976 (AS AMENDED)*

This Act makes it unlawful to discriminate or harass a person on the grounds of race, colour, nationality, or ethnic or national origin, in employment and in the provision of goods, facilities and services.

OCCUPIERS' LIABILITY ACTS 1957 AND 1984

YOUR LIABILITY TO GUESTS AND THE PUBLIC

Under these Acts, the person who controls a premises (the 'occupier') is liable for the physical safety of everyone who comes onto the premises. In some cases, this liability extends to trespassers and other 'uninvited' guests.

Occupiers have what is known as a 'duty of care' to guests and other visitors, and must make sure that the premises are reasonably safe for the purpose for which guests were invited to use them.

This legislation applies to you if you are the owner of a B&B with control over your premises.

WHAT DOES THIS LEGISLATION MEAN IN PRACTICE?

You must make sure that the premises are 'reasonably safe' – for example, that floors are not slippery, passageways are clear, cables are tucked away, furniture and wall fixtures are secure, and that guests have been acquainted with emergency procedures and the layout of the premises, as appropriate.

Your duty of care does not normally extend to parts of your premises that are clearly marked as being out of bounds to guests (such as the kitchens).

Generally, the owner is also liable for accidents caused as a result of the actions of his or her staff, or other guests – for example, if a member of staff leaves a bucket on the stairs and someone trips over it and injures themselves.

No matter how many notices you put up to the contrary, and whatever your booking conditions may say, the law does not allow you to exclude or restrict your liability for death and injuries to guests arising from your negligence (or that of your staff). You can, however, take out insurance to cover your liability.

The duty of care is not entirely one way: each guest has a duty to take care of their own safety. This means that you will not normally be liable for a guest who injures themselves while involved in an activity that a guest might not reasonably have been expected to do on the premises, such as abseiling from an upper-floor window! If their own negligence led to an accident, this would reduce, or could even override, any liability that the owner would otherwise have had.

If anyone makes a claim against you, seek legal advice immediately.

ARE YOU COVERED?

If you start offering serviced accommodation, you need to consider whether you have adequate insurance to cover, for example, your potential liability under the Occupiers' and Employers' Liability Acts. Most household policies will not cover your use of the premises for business purposes, your legal liability to employees or paying guests or any theft or damage to your property by guests. In any event, you should contact your existing insurers as soon as possible.

PUBLIC LIABILITY INSURANCE

One type of insurance cover you should consider, particularly as the general public becomes increasingly claims-conscious, is public liability insurance. This covers your liability to guests and others for injury, loss and damage (for example, under the Occupiers' Liability Acts). There is no legal requirement to take out public liability insurance, but it is a requirement for participation in VisitBritain's National Quality Assessment Schemes.

OTHER TYPES OF INSURANCE

Public liability insurance does not cover loss or damage to proprietors' property, nor should it be confused with employers' liability insurance.

Other regulations that could affect you

- CAN I TURN GUESTS AWAY?
- THE DISABILITY DISCRIMINATION ACT
- TWO OTHER ACTS CONCERNING DISCRIMINATION
- OCCUPIERS' LIABILITY ACTS 1957 AND 1984
- HEALTH AND SAFETY AT WORK ACT 1974
- FOOD SAFETY ACT 1990
- FOOD SAFETY (GENERAL FOOD HYGIENE) REGULATIONS 1995
- TELEVISION LICENCES
- TRADE DESCRIPTIONS ACT 1968
- IMMIGRATION (HOTEL RECORDS) ORDER 1972 (AS AMENDED) – KEEPING A REGISTER OF YOUR GUESTS

TAKING OUT INSURANCE

Some insurance brokers have special insurance packages available for accommodation providers that include public liability insurance, employers' liability insurance, and property and contents insurance. A broker will be able to advise you on these types of comprehensive package, or about adding extra cover to an existing policy.

The insurance broker you use should be a member of the Insurance Brokers' Regulatory Council (IBRC). You will then know that they are properly regulated and subject to a code of conduct.

HEALTH AND SAFETY AT WORK ACT 1974

YOUR RESPONSIBILITIES AS AN EMPLOYER TO EMPLOYEES AND OTHERS

This Act sets the framework for health and safety regulations in the workplace. The Act places general duties and responsibilities on all people at work, including employers, employees and the self-employed. There are two important responsibilities for an employer:

You are responsible for ensuring, so far as is reasonably practicable, the health, safety and welfare of all your employees at work. (Your employees also have a responsibility to take reasonable care of their own health and safety.)

You also have a wider responsibility to ensure, again so far as is reasonably practicable, that you do not put anyone else's health and safety at risk through your work activities – for example, the health and safety of a guest, a casual worker, or a contractor.

You must carry out a risk assessment to identify any risks and then make decisions on how to manage such risks, so far as is reasonably practicable, to comply with health and safety law. If you employ five or more employees, you must record the significant findings of the assessment, and any group of employees it identifies as being especially at risk.

ELECTRICITY AT WORK REGULATIONS 1989

These regulations are wide ranging, but accommodation employers should be aware of one objective in particular: that all electrical systems in places of work must be maintained 'so far as is reasonably practicable' to avoid danger to all who use the premises (including guests).

All electrical systems are covered by the regulations, whether they are used solely by you and your staff, jointly by you, your staff and guests, or solely by your guests.

FOOD SAFETY ACT **1990**

The main requirements regarding food safety are found in the Food Safety Act 1990 and the regulations made under it – particularly those relating to hygiene, temperature control, and labelling.

You must comply with the provisions of the Act if you supply food (which is defined as including drink) to guests.

REGISTRATION

Virtually all accommodation businesses that serve food or drink of any kind are required by the Act to register with their local authority. You do this by completing a simple form that you can obtain from the environmental health department of your local authority. Registration is free and the local authority cannot refuse to register your premises.

There is an exemption that rarely applies (Food Premises (Registration) Regulations 1991). If you live on the premises and offer accommodation in no more than three bedrooms, and the sale of any food and drink is secondary to the provision of the accommodation, you do not have to register. This exemption is aimed at those people who offer accommodation only, but who may provide tea and biscuits. It is not available to those who offer proper bed and breakfast.

New businesses must register at least 28 days before they open for business. You must also notify the registration authorities of a change of proprietor and of the nature of a food business.

Other regulations that could affect you

- CAN I TURN GUESTS AWAY?

- THE DISABILITY DISCRIMINATION ACT

- TWO OTHER ACTS CONCERNING DISCRIMINATION

- OCCUPIERS' LIABILITY ACTS 1957 AND 1984

- HEALTH AND SAFETY AT WORK ACT 1974

- FOOD SAFETY ACT 1990

- FOOD SAFETY (GENERAL FOOD HYGIENE) REGULATIONS 1995

- TELEVISION LICENCES

- TRADE DESCRIPTIONS ACT 1968

- IMMIGRATION (HOTEL RECORDS) ORDER 1972 (AS AMENDED) – KEEPING A REGISTER OF YOUR GUESTS

The main provisions of the Act concentrate on what you must *not* do. There are four main offences:

(a)   Selling, or possessing for sale, food which does not comply with food safety requirements

The food safety requirements are that food must not have been rendered injurious to health. This means that it must not have been treated, prepared or kept in a way that has made it harmful to health, for example because of anything that has been added to it, or because of any ingredients used in it. Food must also not be unfit (rotten or 'gone off') or so contaminated, whether by outside substances or otherwise, that it would be unreasonable to expect it to be eaten.

(b)   Rendering food injurious to health

Not only is it an offence to sell food that is harmful to health, it is also an offence to do anything that would make food harmful by adding something to it or removing something from it. This applies even if you did not realise the effect of what you were doing at the time.

(c)   Selling, to the purchaser's prejudice, food which is not of the nature, substance or quality demanded

'To the purchaser's prejudice' means to his or her disadvantage. This includes things like supplying regular lemonade when low-calorie lemonade has been requested, or supplying a beef casserole when the customer has ordered lamb casserole.

(d)   Falsely or misleadingly describing, advertising or presenting food

This offence can be committed when statements or pictures concerning food are misleading. It can also cover statements that are strictly correct, but presented in such a way that the customer is led to the wrong conclusion. With this in mind, you should take care with the descriptions of dishes on your menus.

INSPECTIONS

Local environmental health officers and trading standards officers have the right to enter and inspect food premises (registered or not) at any reasonable time, and they do not need to make an appointment. They carry out routine inspections, and the frequency of their inspections varies depending on the degree of risk posed by the business and its previous record. Inspectors may also visit as the result of a complaint.

FOOD SAFETY (GENERAL FOOD HYGIENE) REGULATIONS 1995

These general food hygiene regulations illustrate how food legislation is moving away from prescriptive, detailed requirements to a more common-sense approach, where controls are related to the degree of risk. In principle, therefore, the lower the risk, the lower the level of safeguards needed.

You must comply with the regulations if you are an accommodation provider who offers food to guests. It does not matter whether you are a small B&B or a five-star hotel.

HOW DO YOU COMPLY?

There is a general requirement to ensure that all food operations are carried out in a hygienic way. As a basic requirement, food premises must

be kept clean, be well maintained and designed to enable good hygiene practices to be adhered to

have adequate hand-washing facilities available, with supplies of hot and cold water, and drying facilities suitably located and designated for cleaning hands (toilets must not open directly into rooms where food is handled)

have adequate means of ventilation, lighting and drainage.

What is adequate in any situation will depend on the nature and size of the business. However, it is prudent to look at the requirements of the Act in detail.

Other regulations that could affect you

- CAN I TURN GUESTS AWAY?

- THE DISABILITY DISCRIMINATION ACT

- TWO OTHER ACTS CONCERNING DISCRIMINATION

- OCCUPIERS' LIABILITY ACTS 1957 AND 1984

- HEALTH AND SAFETY AT WORK ACT 1974

- FOOD SAFETY ACT 1990

- FOOD SAFETY (GENERAL FOOD HYGIENE) REGULATIONS 1995

- TELEVISION LICENCES

- TRADE DESCRIPTIONS ACT 1968

- IMMIGRATION (HOTEL RECORDS) ORDER 1972 (AS AMENDED) – KEEPING A REGISTER OF YOUR GUESTS

TELEVISION LICENCES

You should apply for a Hotel and Mobile Units Television Licence ('hotel licence') if you offer short-stay accommodation to overnight visitors and have installed television sets in your guest rooms. You should also note that, despite its name, the 'hotel licence' includes B&Bs.

The TV Licensing Authority says that you should always take out a hotel licence if you are providing televisions for the use of guests. While staying on your property, guests are not covered by their home licence.

The fee for the licence is determined by the number of guest rooms or guest units in which you have installed or intend to install television sets. If this number is no more than 15, the fee is the same as a standard domestic licence fee.

The hotel licence is available only from TV Licensing. All enquiries should be addressed to: Hotel Licensing Centre, TV Licensing, Bristol, BS98 1TL (tel: 0117 373 6209).

TRADE DESCRIPTIONS ACT 1968

This legislation applies to you if you either advertise your accommodation facilities in a brochure or any other form of advertising material (including the web) or make statements about your facilities to the public.

WHAT DOES THE ACT COVER?

This Act states that it is an offence for you, knowingly or recklessly, to make 'false statements' about any facilities or services offered by you. False statements relating to accommodation facilities could include statements made about the quality, amenities and location of the accommodation premises or services related to it. It would, for example, be a false statement if you advertised that your accommodation was 'five minutes from the beach' when it is in fact a half-hour drive, or that 'the rooms are spacious with panoramic views' when this description applies to one room only.

Equally, the display of a sign or logo to which you are not entitled could constitute a false statement. For example, if you were to display on your premises an incorrect

VisitBritain rating, or an outdated Tourist Board rating such as a Crown classification and grading, this could be regarded as a breach of the Act.

IMMIGRATION (HOTEL RECORDS) ORDER 1972 (AS AMENDED) – KEEPING A REGISTER OF YOUR GUESTS

All B&B accommodation premises must keep a record of all guests over the age of 16 under this Order. This means that you will need to record:

* for all guests, on arrival, their full name and nationality
* for all non-British, Irish or Commonwealth guests, on arrival, their passport number and place of issue (or other document which shows their identity and nationality)
* for all guests who are not either British, Irish or from Commonwealth countries, on or before departure, details of their next destination (including the address, if known).

Diplomats and their family and staff do not have to register. You do not have to ask for a guest's home address.

The register does not need to be in any set format. It could be a visitors' book or an exercise book, but you must keep each guest's details for at least 12 months, and have the register available for inspection by a police officer or duly authorised person at all times.

It may be, of course, that you are given the necessary details at the time of booking, but you should check them when the guests arrive and make sure that you have all the information you are required to collect. Even if your local police have traditionally shown no interest in these records, circumstances could change.

Next steps

Now that you are aware of the regulations and have worked through the process of establishing the suitability of your property, you can start to plan your venture. You may already have decided on the number of rooms you want to let out. Indeed, this may have been determined by the fire regulations detailed above. In this respect, it is no

Other regulations that could affect you

- CAN I TURN GUESTS AWAY?
- THE DISABILITY DISCRIMINATION ACT
- TWO OTHER ACTS CONCERNING DISCRIMINATION
- OCCUPIERS' LIABILITY ACTS 1957 AND 1984
- HEALTH AND SAFETY AT WORK ACT 1974
- FOOD SAFETY ACT 1990
- FOOD SAFETY (GENERAL FOOD HYGIENE) REGULATIONS 1995
- TELEVISION LICENCES
- TRADE DESCRIPTIONS ACT 1968
- IMMIGRATION (HOTEL RECORDS) ORDER 1972 (AS AMENDED) – KEEPING A REGISTER OF YOUR GUESTS

Next steps

coincidence that the majority of B&Bs accommodate no more than six guests. Beyond six bed spaces, properties can be affected by a number of laws, as this chapter has detailed, which is why most B&Bs conform to what is called the 'six bed space rule'.

You will also have an idea of the market you hope to attract, and the standard that you want to achieve. All this information should help you decide where you want to position yourself and in turn will guide you into not making costly mistakes while getting your property equipped and ready.

The next chapter details how you should go about launching your property. It looks at what you should consider when preparing the B&B, letting the rooms, advertising, and getting graded.

Chapter 4

Launching the operation

You now have the necessary planning permission (if it was required) and are confident that you are aware of and will meet all the legal requirements. Now you can go ahead with the exciting task of converting, adapting and equipping your B&B. However, before you get deep into organising builders, thinking of interior design features and buying bedlinen and teapots, there is another priority issue to start working on.

Preparing the B&B

QUALITY STANDARD

It is important at this stage to consider the overall quality standard you are trying to achieve. There are more details of VisitBritain's National Quality Assurance Scheme (NQAS) for Guest Accommodation, which includes B&Bs, later in this chapter. This is a grading scheme that awards ratings according to quality, on the basis that the higher the quality of the accommodation, the higher the rating.

Distribution of quality ratings in NQAS Guest Accommodation

1 Star	0.5%
2 Star	4%
3 Star	39%
4 Star	52%
5 Star	4.5%

Note: All ratings have been expressed as Stars as these are replacing Diamonds
Source: VisitBritain   Nov 2005

It helps to decide on the quality rating you would like and then work towards it. The rating will depend on many factors, both tangible and intangible, including the quality of beds and bedding, style and quality of furniture, and spaciousness of rooms. The quality of breakfast, hospitality and cleanliness will also have a bearing on the rating. All of these points are assessed in more detail later, but it is worth asking whether you want to be a top quality B&B. The answer is, of course, yes. However, you need to be realistic and ask yourself whether in fact your property might not appeal more to the middle market, which is possibly an easier price to achieve.

SOME INITIAL CONSIDERATIONS

Some of the initial points that you should consider are parking and entrances. For many visitors, safe parking is becoming a necessity. You may be able to provide this if your property has a large garden, with a sufficient parking area for you and your guests. If, however, you have only a limited off-street area, could you create more space or park your own vehicles elsewhere?

When guests arrive, will they use the same entrance door as you and the family? If guests have to climb over personal belongings, this may not create the 'welcome' and positive first impression that you will have hoped to convey. And, if you have a young family, this may not be convenient for them and you either, and it might be better for guests to arrive by a separate entrance door, assuming you have one. If you cannot do this, you could move the family entrance to the back of the property, and have the guests' entrance at the front.

WHAT TYPES OF ROOM SHOULD YOU HAVE?

If your children have left home and you are using existing beds, then you may already have decided what type of room you are going for. However, if you plan to replace beds or equip the B&B from scratch, you will need to take into account the number of rooms that you are planning to let in order to have the best flexibility. What you are looking for is the best combination of beds and types of rooms: if you are planning to let three rooms, for example it would be uneconomical to have just three single beds.

All of this will, of course, depend on the size of your rooms. If your rooms have space for two single beds, then a twin-room arrangement is very flexible. A twin room can accommodate a single guest, two guests travelling together, or possibly a couple. Zip-and-link beds increase the flexibility of a twin room. They are more expensive, but they offer the best option because they allow a twin room to be converted into a very comfortable double room, creating a king-sized double bed when the two single beds are zipped together.

However, twin rooms need more extra space than double-bedded rooms do, to allow for manoeuvring beside and between the beds. If the bedroom is not too spacious, you may need to consider keeping it as a double. And then consider whether the room will accommodate a standard double bed (4ft 6in wide), a queen bed (5ft) or even a king-sized bed (6ft). A standard size single bed is 3ft wide.

If you are keeping within the six-bed-space rule, then a suitable combination could be two twin bedrooms and a double bedroom. This can offer the best flexibility for you when it comes to letting the accommodation.

BATHROOMS

The next decision you need to make is how to organise your bathrooms. If you have a property where there is only one bathroom available, your guests will have to share it with your family. This arrangement is still acceptable within VisitBritain's National Quality Assurance Schemes (but within certain limits – you should consult the NQAS standard for more information), but it is becoming less common. However, this arrangement puts extra constraints on your family: they will, for example, have to remove all personal belongings from the bathroom when there are guests using it as well. In a smaller property – with just one person running the B&B who can maintain standards more easily – this arrangement can work quite well, but in a household with a whole family, including children, this situation is going to become less easy to manage and less convenient for everyone, especially the guest. It can, in effect, be quite impractical.

If you have three bedrooms but only one shared bathroom, you could convert one room into another bathroom. The demand for an en suite or private bathroom is increasing, and sometimes the first question potential guests ask when looking for accommodation is whether you offer this facility. If, however, you cannot create a large en suite or you do not want to lose the additional income a third bedroom could generate, you could consider creating an en suite bathroom within an existing bedroom (providing, of course, you have the space). This is likely to be quite a large building project, as waste pipes will need to be extended and additional plumbing will be required. However, it could create a convenient long-term solution, which would also help with your lettings – you can usually charge more for a room with an en suite or private bathroom than for one with a shared bathroom.

DECORATING THE BEDROOMS

You need to get the balance right when you decorate your rooms. Emulsion may be easier to maintain than wallpaper, and it could be relatively easy to add interest with special paint effects or relief. You could also use colour to play tricks on the eye: painting a high ceiling in a dark colour can make it appear lower, and using a dark colour on opposite walls can make a wide room seem narrower. It is also easier, and less expensive, to use paint to change the appearance of a room, should you want to refresh the decoration or merely to change colours to suit current fashions.

Wall coverings can be patterned, embossed or textured, but should all be of a type that can be damp-wiped. Textured, finished wallpaper will have the benefit of helping to disguise slightly irregular wall and ceiling surfaces, something that is especially useful in older properties. As wallpaper can get scuffed easily, it will be important to keep a spare roll for any repairs that become necessary.

Adding skirting boards will protect the walls from damage by furniture or a vacuum cleaner. In a similar way, a dado rail will protect a wall from knocks from the back of a chair, while also providing a natural break in the wall's colour scheme. Mirrors help the room feel larger, and provide a useful accessory for guests. Picture rails can be effective in allowing pictures to be moved around easily without requiring more holes to be knocked in the wall; they also provide a visual break in rooms with high ceilings. And pictures can provide the finishing touch, adding character and interest and reinforcing the sense of the B&B's location: in a rural B&B, for example, the pictures may all be local scenes.

DECORATING THE BATHROOMS

Make sure to use suitable wall coverings when you are decorating the bathrooms. People using bathrooms create a hotter and steamier environment, and condensation and damp can be problems. A first option could be to install an extractor fan, which should help reduce condensation, and make it a lot easier to keep the bathroom clean.

The walls and floors will sometimes require regular washing and wiping. Most emulsion paints have dedicated ranges that are specifically appropriate for bathrooms. Fully tiled walls are easier to maintain, but it will be very important to ensure that they have been properly grouted. If all-over tiling is not appropriate, perhaps because of the composition of the wall, it could be useful to have tiled splashbacks immediately above the basin and bath.

EQUIPPING THE BEDROOM

When you are thinking about what to provide for your guests, spend time making sure that everything can be used with ease. We will look at the way in which guests use their accommodation in greater detail in Chapter 6, but at this stage you need to consider how the room will be designed, where the bed will be positioned, and where the wardrobe and other furniture will be placed. Having done that, you will need to consider the location of lights, switches and power points.

POWER POINTS

Try not to skimp on the number of power points when planning or preparing the bedrooms. Adding these later is almost always more expensive and disruptive, so consider who may be staying and what their requirements are likely to be. In most guest bedrooms you will find a kettle, television, bedside lights, table lights, and maybe a clock radio. In addition, many B&Bs provide a hair dryer and allow guests to borrow an iron and ironing board. A fan may be useful for the hot summer months. And remember that the business guest may have a laptop and a printer, and may want to recharge their mobile phone.

As you can see, the more power points there are, the better (about six should suffice), but they must always be placed for maximum convenience. There is nothing worse than having to move furniture just to be able to plug in the kettle and make a cup of tea.

STORAGE SPACE

The overall space available and the needs of the guests staying will determine what type of storage you provide in a bedroom. Some visitors will stay only one night and may not unpack at all – but is there somewhere for their luggage to be placed? A business traveller who also only stays for one night may not want to live out of a suitcase, so will need hanging space for their jacket and skirt or trousers, and shelf storage for other items. Freestanding wardrobes and chests of drawers can take up valuable space, but can, if of a very high quality, give a room an improved appearance. Built-in furniture and open-plan clothes organisers can provide suitable alternatives, although their intrinsic quality may be lower. There are now major retailers who specialise in 'storage solutions'.

USE OF THE ROOM

Consider the location of lights and switches. As well as a main overhead light or fixed wall lights, you may also want to provide standard and table lamps. You should have bedside lights by the bed, possibly wall-fixed lights at a suitable height (whichever type of lighting you use, set it at a height that allows for reading in bed, in comfort). You could also provide a main light switch by the bed so guests can turn the bedroom lights on and off from their bed.

Bedside tables or shelves will be useful, but think about their size. If they are too small, or cluttered with other accessories, the guest will have nowhere to put what could be classed the essentials: a pair of glasses, a book, a glass of water, a watch (and maybe the TV remote).

GUEST LOUNGE

A B&B does not need to have a guest lounge – which will be good news for you if you feel that you do not have a spare room that can be used as a dedicated guests' lounge, or that you do not want to share your own lounge with the guests. Indeed, in some circumstances a ground-floor room would be better used as bedroom accommodation. However, without a guest lounge you must provide comfortable chairs in the bedrooms if you wish to be quality assured.

If you do have space, however, it is worth thinking about creating a guest lounge. In some circumstances a guest lounge can be a very useful facility, especially for guests on holiday or attending a function. It provides a place to relax and meet friends before going out. The room does not have to be large; you can have space for easy seating even in a small room. And you should bear in mind that, if you are thinking about making your own sitting room available to guests, it does not necessarily have to be available all day. You just need to make sure that guests know which room it is (although keeping the door open will help them realise that it also for their use) and when they can use it.

DINING ROOM

Give some thought to which room or area you will use for the dining room. In some farmhouse B&Bs breakfast may be served in a large farmhouse kitchen. In some more modern properties, the breakfast room is also the lounge, but is set up late in the evening or at night. Where space allows, the breakfast room could be a separate room.

Whichever room you use, it is worth thinking about how you will seat your guests. Will it be around one large table, or will you use separate tables? Accommodating all your guests around one table can work really well, as this will often help stimulate conversation. Small tables can provide more space for each guest, and can make for ease of service. Either arrangement can be effective, but each can also provide difficulties. In Chapter 7 we shall look at the pros and cons of each option, and some simple ideas to make each work well.

If you plan to use tablecloths you will require more linen, which will incur additional laundry costs. When choosing crockery and cutlery, think about whether you plan to hand-wash everything – if you do not, choose items that are dishwasher-proof – and what design of crockery you will use. If you choose from a limited design range, it may not be easy to replace any items that get broken. You may also need to purchase serving dishes, coffee pots and tea pots, glasses and jugs, cutlery, and other items for the breakfast table, such as coasters, table mats and salt and pepper sets.

KITCHEN

It is easy to think that all the changes needed in a B&B will be to the guests' areas. True, you will need to equip the bedrooms and bathrooms and consider changes in the lounge and dining rooms – all the areas where guests go. But you will also need to think about your own private areas as well. The kitchen will need to cope with additional food preparation, cooking and washing. You may also need to invest in larger or commercial-style equipment, such as a larger refrigerator, freezer, pots and pans, toaster, kettle, washing machine, tumble-dryer and iron. Indeed, you may prefer to purchase an ironing machine to press larger sheets, pillowcases and tablecloths.

Advertising and promoting your B&B

The rooms are not finished, let alone started on, so why should you think about advertising? Advertising can be very costly, and it would be foolish to spend a fortune now; you may even be inclined to think it is not sensible to do any advertising at all at this early stage. After all, it is only when you are up and running that you will you be able to work out exactly how your guests found out about you. But how do you make potential visitors aware that your establishment exists and will be open for business, even if only in six months' time? Is there anyone in the tourism field who can help you?

HOW IS TOURISM MANAGED IN ENGLAND?

If you are thinking about starting a B&B, you may think that the first place to go for advice would be the Tourist Board. It is a common misassumption that there is one national organisation only that looks after tourism, but there are in fact many organisations involved in promoting tourism and helping the industry. These organisations vary in size – and, variously, promote national, regional and local tourism – but all work closely together.

The national tourism organisation in Britain is VisitBritain (VB). It has an integral arm in England, known as Enjoy England, which works in the home and overseas markets. VB works in conjunction with the Visit Wales, Visit Scotland and the Northern Ireland Tourist Boards. Its principal role is to promote Britain, but it also promotes and helps to develop quality (for example, through the NQAS), and carries out research in support of those functions in England.

The responsibility for regional tourism rests with England's Regional Development Agencies (RDA). Each agency has a tourism section within its own structure or a sister organisation that it works with – the pattern varies a little from region to region. The different regions of England work in slightly different ways, and each has its own priorities, which depend on the nature of tourism in that particular region.

Your first stop should be with your local TIC, which is likely to be run by your local authority. Your TIC may, in turn, direct you for more advice to a regional Tourism Officer, to the RDA's tourism department or to the Regional Tourist Board (although not all regions in England have a Regional Tourist Board – many of these are now part of their RDA).

ACCOMMODATION GUIDES

The major guidebooks – such as VisitBritain's Enjoy England official guides to quality series, and your local accommodation brochures and guides – have lead times before printing, as do all other publications. These times will vary but may be as much as five months before the publication date for the larger guides. This means that, if you miss the deadline, you will not be able to promote your B&B for another year.

VisitBritain and many local authorities produce annual accommodation guides, which are linked to their websites. To advertise with these organisations, you need to have your property assessed under the NQAS. VisitBritain's Quality Assurance Scheme (QAS) assure visitors that the advertised accommodation meets a recognised standard; the ratings assure the visitor of a recognised national standard, and give an indication of levels of quality.

Your property, however, is not ready, so how can you be included in these guides? Well, if you have paid for an assessment, you will be eligible to have details of your accommodation included in the listing. Beside your entry in the guide, instead of a rating, will be the words 'applied for' or 'awaiting assessment', or similar. This clearly shows to any prospective visitor that you intend to become assessed and rated. If you are confident of your opening date, you could even include the date or 'opening at Easter', or something similar.

As a participant in VisitBritain's Quality Assurance Schemes, you receive a free entry in the Enjoy England official guides to quality series and free listing at www.visitbritain.com and www.enjoyengland.com, the official tourism websites for Britain.

Being quality assessed usually allows you an entry in regional guides and local accommodation guides. Produced by local authorities or regional or sub-regional tourism bodies, these cover specific areas, and there are usually associated costs. You may also consider advertising in paid-for guides and specialist magazines, or in national newspapers. If you are aiming to attract specific or specialist markets (such as walkers, cyclists or bird-watchers), you may want to take out a small advert in a relevant publication.

A significant downside in any advertising is that you may be contacted by a number of other publications (such as magazines and newspapers), which will try to persuade you to advertise with them. At this early stage in your business, it will probably be more cost-effective to be selective with your advertising budget.

BROCHURES

In the early stages of developing your B&B, it may seem too expensive to have a full-colour brochure produced professionally. In addition, your rooms or facilities may still be in the process of being decorated and equipped, so you may not be able to photograph them. A stop-gap solution could be to produce your own brochure on a personal computer, possibly with line drawings – this could be very effective, and will cost relatively little.

A more professional brochure is something you might consider once the property is completed and there are fewer immediate calls on your money. What information should you include in such a brochure, and how will it be used?

The first piece of information will be the B&B's name. If it does not already have one, you may need to think of one – names can be important, and can be used as a marketing tool. If you are thinking of a fresh name for your establishment, try to think of the impression it will convey. Hill View, for example, can create an image of a countryside location; The Old Rectory may be exactly what your property is; The Rowans may refer precisely to the trees that dominate the garden. Whatever you choose, the visitor will always find it easier to remember a name than a street address. It is important to realise that businesses with 'hotel' in their name will be assessed accordingly and not as a B&B.

Include photographs illustrating the accommodation in your brochure, and any special features, such as a log fireplace, a landscaped garden, or the view from the bedroom window. A short description of the bedrooms, such as 'one ground floor double-bedded en suite' and 'one twin-bedded with private bathroom and views of garden' can help to sell the B&B. A location map, with simple, easy-to-follow directions – and visual aids along the route – is very useful. Remember, guests may arrive at night, and they will welcome anything that helps them find you easily. Rather than specify mile distances from a junction, give advice such as 'turn right at the Crown Pub', or 'left at the post office'.

Distances that you should specify, however, are those of your establishment from places of interest. Being just off a major road may appeal to business travellers; proximity to a tourist attraction may be a draw for guests on a break. Being one mile from the M1, or a five-minute drive from the coast can all be used to good effect.

The tariff is very important, and dating the information is a consideration. If you plan to use the brochure for a long period, you could have the tariff on a separate insert, but this will involve additional costs, and there are anyway two views on this. Many small operators do not like to quote prices in print, preferring to agree the rate at the time of the booking. However, an indication of the price, or the range of rates, is something a potential guest will be looking for.

Think about how your brochure will be used before deciding on its size. Many B&B brochures are sent in the post in response to requests for information, so the brochure will need to fit into an envelope; the most suitable sized envelope is a DL, or 11x22cm-sized envelope. These take a single sheet of A4 paper folded into three. By designing your brochure as a three-fold A4 sheet, you will not need to buy special envelopes. In addition, this will enable you to post out complimentary print material to guests, such as local events and attractions leaflets, which are often produced in the same format.

Business cards can be very useful, too, if given to guests on departure or distributed to places such as local pubs, tearooms, garages, other B&Bs, and hotels and local shops.

WEBSITE

More and more people are looking for accommodation on the internet, which will often be the first point of research for prospective guests, since it allows them to view details of many properties, as opposed to making individual phone enquiries. Guests will nowadays want to see pictures of the accommodation, information on the B&B, including rates, and will possibly want to e-mail you with an enquiry. This allows them to make a more informed decision on where to stay, and to book their accommodation more easily

One of the many benefits of a website is that it can be updated within a short time, and you will be able to add photographs of the rooms as they become ready. While on the subject of photographs, aim to use photographs of the accommodation on your website, as well as general photographs of the area. After all, although you are selling the accommodation in the first instance, you are selling your location as well.

Setting up your own site may prove costly if you have to use a web designer. It is worth looking around, and talking to people, to see if there is cheaper expertise that you could use.

Obtaining your grading

Your B&B has now been planned, you have settled on the mix of rooms, the set-up of the dining room, the general style of decoration and the style of furniture, and have begun thinking about promoting your property. What you need to do next is to think about being assessed and graded.

The following section describes how VisitBritain's QAS operate, and how the assessment is carried out. Being quality assessed is a very positive and constructive exercise, providing you with a lot of helpful and important advice at an early stage, as well as the marketing opportunities that only VisitBritain can offer.

THE NATIONAL QUALITY ASSURANCE SCHEME (NQAS)

As has been said above, you will need to have been awarded a quality rating if you want to promote your property in any of the publications produced by VisitBritain, or by many local authorities and tourism organisations.

The only two organisations currently to carry out assessments in England are VisitBritain and the AA. Both assess B&Bs in the same way, working to a common, harmonised standard, which is consistent throughout England, Scotland and Wales.

Advertising and promoting your B&B

- HOW IS TOURISM MANAGED IN ENGLAND?
- ACCOMMODATION GUIDES
- BROCHURES
- WEBSITE

Obtaining your grading

- THE NATIONAL QUALITY ASSURANCE SCHEME (NQAS)
- WHAT ARE THE BENEFITS OF BEING ASSESSED?
- HOW DO YOU OBTAIN A RATING?
- WHAT HAPPENS NEXT?
- WHAT IS THE ASSESSOR LOOKING FOR?
- HOW DO THE FIVE RATINGS DIFFER?
- WHO ASSESSES?

WHAT ARE THE BENEFITS OF BEING ASSESSED?

There are two main benefits to being assessed by VisitBritain, which can be divided into the areas of marketing and management.

THE MARKETING BENEFITS

Marketing benefits include being able to show a quality rating – an official and independent endorsement from the official tourism body for Britain – alongside your business. A rating provides your customers with the assurance that you are meeting and maintaining quality standards, both in terms of physical quality and in the areas that customers find most important, such as cleanliness, hospitality and food quality.

In addition, your B&B will receives free listing in the Enjoy England official guides to quality, the national guides for accommodation in England, and on VisitBritain's national website. This listing is available to over 560 TICs in England, each of which receives hundreds of enquiries each day. The listing is also provided to all VisitBritain offices overseas.

You can use the quality rating on your brochures, website, any advertising you do, and on signage and stationery.

THE MANAGEMENT BENEFITS

The management benefits are the expert advice you receive from one of VisitBritain's quality assessors. Each assessor sees more than 300 establishments a year, and can offer advice on developing your B&B. The advice is not prescriptive – you don't have to take suggested actions if you don't want to. The assessor's role is to assess where your operation sits in relation to a national rating. However, they are also there to discuss ideas and make suggestions based on what they have seen and experienced at other B&Bs. The assessment becomes a very effective way of sharing best practice.

HOW DO YOU OBTAIN A RATING?

To achieve a rating, you will first need to contact Quality In Tourism (see details below), which carries out assessments on behalf of VisitBritain. A fee will be charged, based on the number of rooms you have and the rate you charge for a one-night stay. (The good news is that when the assessor comes to stay, they pay for their accommodation.)

The assessment should take place within approximately eight weeks of Quality In Tourism acknowledging your application. In this time, the assessor will be assigned the visit, and they will attempt to book a night at your B&B. Should your B&B be full for the night they ask for, they will try again at a later date.

WHAT HAPPENS NEXT?
The assessor, having made a booking, will stay just like any other guest, using the room, having breakfast and paying their bill. Once the bill is paid, they will announce who they are and ask if you can spare some time for the assessment debrief.

They will then spend time looking at the other bedrooms and at any other public areas they would not have seen during their stay. Their role is twofold: first, to ensure that you get the right grading for your B&B; and secondly, to provide advice on developing quality. The points raised in this second stage are advisory, not compulsory. The only thing you must do after any assessment is meet minimum standards. Should you not meet one or more of the minimum standards, these will form part of a written report that you will be required to act upon before the next assessment.

After the visit, you will receive confirmation of the grade your establishment has achieved, the written quality assessment report and a certificate.

WHAT IS THE ASSESSOR LOOKING FOR?
The first thing the assessor is looking for is the reassurance that all properties meet the requirements for minimum standards. As quality standards increase beyond this minimum level, so the star rating will increase, and, from 2008, all B&Bs will be graded from one to five stars.

Minimum standards relate to the basic requirements for facilities and services and cover issues that will include cleanliness, being fit for purpose, having lights, providing a bath mat in the bathroom and ensuring there is a good range of items available at breakfast. The standards booklet for B&Bs lists all the minimum requirements for the NQAS. For a copy of the booklet, contact Quality in Tourism on 0845 3006996, or email qualityintourism@gslglobal.com

Case Study
An Inspector Calls

We are often referred to as 'inspectors', but a more accurate description would be 'assessors'. The very idea of inspecting something carries the notion of seeing if something is 'up to standard', and criticising it if it's not. That's not what we are about. I, along with a team of colleagues, will assess a property as it stands and operates, awarding a rating based on the quality of the property and its position in the marketplace.

You cannot tell if something is good unless you have seen a range of properties, and a major part of our training involves seeing all sorts of establishment. These range from those with a basic acceptable standard through to the truly excellent. Standards are set by the industry and based on the customer's expectations. There is no way that I could make an assessment unless I had seen, and experienced, what now runs to hundreds of different establishments.

What happens on an assessment? It begins before I arrive. Every initial assessment involves an overnight stay, and I telephone and book a room just like any other guest. Everything has an element of quality to it, even the way in which a call and booking is handled. The guest does not expect a 'hotel' standard, but establishments vary in how efficiently they deal with these calls and in their telephone manner (friendly or otherwise), and I'll note what happens compared to other like establishments.

How the guest is dealt with on arrival and when given an 'informed welcome' can have quite an impact, and this

continued

would be another area that I will note, along with the quality of all aspects of the accommodation. This does not only mean the intrinsic and physical quality but also the thought that has been put into considering the comfort and convenience of the guest. Again, the assessment is based on comparison with the best practice in other like B&Bs.

Plenty of exercise helps me to cope with my fair share of breakfasts! These are an important part of the B&B formula and they need to meet the expectation of different guests with different tastes and dietary requirements, even though these will often be very similar. I do not make a habit of asking for the unusual, but I do observe what other guests are requesting, and how those requests are dealt with.

After I've paid my bill, I'll say who I am and I usually manage to see any other bedrooms. What follows after that is often the best bit of the assessment for both me and the operator. I debrief on all aspects of my stay, literally from beginning to end. There are always some really good quality points, and it's very rewarding to recognise and acknowledge these. However, what may also come from the debrief are the identification of areas where quality could be enhanced and developed further, often at low cost and to the potential benefit of guest and operator alike. It's important to note that quality recommendations are 'could-do' and not 'must-do'. The last thing I want to do is tell an operator how to run their business. We work in partnership and do not 'police' the industry. One thing, however, that I and a lot of B&B operators have come to appreciate is that things are always changing and developing, because quality, like the customers' expectations, never stands still. Any recommendations are based on other examples from similar operators, not on personal opinions. It's amazing how objective you become in this job. I didn't think that would be the case when I first became an assessor (as a poacher turned gamekeeper).

Obtaining your grading

- THE NATIONAL QUALITY ASSURANCE SCHEME (NQAS)
- WHAT ARE THE BENEFITS OF BEING ASSESSED?
- HOW DO YOU OBTAIN A RATING?
- WHAT HAPPENS NEXT?
- WHAT IS THE ASSESSOR LOOKING FOR?
- HOW DO THE FIVE RATINGS DIFFER?
- WHO ASSESSES?

continued

61

> I put the points that we have discussed into a written
> report for the operator, which they receive along with
> their certificate giving their rating after the visit. This
> rating helps tell the visitor that you are just what they are
> looking for.

HOW DO THE FIVE RATINGS DIFFER?

The following provide only a rough guide; the Guest
Accomodation Quality Standard booklet provides more
comprehensive information.

1 STAR

Simple, practical, no-frills accommodation suitable for those
on a tight budget. Decor will be clean and furnishings fit for
purpose. Beds will be made up with clean linen and bedding;
towels and soap are provided. Bedrooms will have a form
of heating, acceptable light levels, and privacy. Bathroom
facilities may be shared, with hot water available at reasonable
times. As a minimum, breakfast will be provided – either a
full cooked meal or, if notified in advance, a substantial
continental breakfast. Service levels may be limited.

2 STARS

Well presented and well run accommodation offering a
modest level of quality, but with some facility and service
enhancements, such as in-room televisions and fitted
heating. Decor will be in good condition, and furnishings
sound and usable. Each room will be provided with
well-positioned lighting. Floorings will provide adequate
comfort underfoot. Bath or shower rooms may be en suite or
shared. Facilities will be maintained in a clean and serviceable
condition. Additional services might be provided, such as
dinner. Meals may be simple, with limited choice, but must
be freshly prepared.

3 STARS

Accommodation offering a good overall level of quality and
comfort in all areas. Bedrooms will offer a reasonable amount
of space and comfort. Decor will show some co-ordination
with the soft furnishings. Furniture will be fairly substantial,

and may provide additional facilities, such as a writing desk. Good quality co-ordinated carpeting, curtains and seating will be provided, as well as conveniently positioned lighting and controlled heating. En suite facilities, where provided, may be compact, but will be clean and well maintained, and all other rooms will have washbasins. Soap and toiletries will be provided. A wider selection may be offered at breakfast, including a choice of eggs cooked to order. Service throughout will be efficient and hospitable. Good levels of service and guest care will be evident.

4 STARS

Accommodation offering an excellent quality in all areas. Bedrooms will be more spacious, with a special emphasis on quality of decor, furnishings, fixtures and fittings. Extra facilities and personal touches may be provided, such as a hairdryer or radio. At least half the bedrooms will have en suite or private facilities, which will be well fitted with quality sanitary ware, effective lighting and ventilation. Towelling will be of high quality, and a range of toiletry items will be provided. A very good breakfast will be offered, with a wide selection of starter and cooked options. Local specialities may be featured, with an emphasis on fresh ingredients. Service and guest care will be attentive and efficient throughout all areas of the establishment.

5 STARS

Exceptional quality accommodation with a degree of luxury and attentive hospitality. Bedrooms will offer ample space with excellent comfort levels and elements of luxury. High quality decor, furnishings and fittings will feature in all guest areas. Bathroom facilities will be either en suite or private, and fitted out with high quality sanitary ware and fixtures. Luxury towelling, including bath sheets and a wide range of quality toiletries. Public areas will reflect the same high quality as the bedrooms, and provide guests with additional space for comfort and relaxation. Breakfast will offer a wide selection of produce, including quality juices, fruits in season, bakery items and homemade preserves. Cooked options may be numerous, possibly with some original or local specialities. Service and hospitality will be exemplary.

Obtaining your grading

- THE NATIONAL QUALITY ASSURANCE SCHEME (NQAS)

- WHAT ARE THE BENEFITS OF BEING ASSESSED?

- HOW DO YOU OBTAIN A RATING?

- WHAT HAPPENS NEXT?

- WHAT IS THE ASSESSOR LOOKING FOR?

- HOW DO THE FIVE RATINGS DIFFER?

- WHO ASSESSES?

WHO ASSESSES?

Assessors come from an industry background, to ensure they have an understanding and empathy with the industry and the guests' expectations. They undertake comprehensive training, which includes an annual seminar and individual one-to-one accompanied training. Throughout the year, they receive further accompanied assessments. The detailed training programme helps to ensure that assessors are all working to the same objective standards.

In the next three chapters we will look at the visitor journey from initial enquiry through to departure. Chapter 5 will cover what happens before the guest arrives, and on arrival. Chapter 6 will look at the guest's stay in relation to the bedrooms and bathroom, and Chapter 7 will look at breakfast and departure.

Chapter 5

'Its not what you do, it's the way that you do it'

Enquiry and arrival

The next three chapters focus on the guest's journey from their initial telephone enquiry, through to their departure at the end of their stay with you. This chapter will look at telephone enquiries, examining the way in which an enquiry is handled and how this can enhance or detract from first impressions. We look at different examples of best practice, how an enquiry can be converted into a booking, and how to develop repeat and referral business. We also look at the guest's arrival, and at many ideas that can help make their first impression as positive as possible – you can after all make a first impression only once. We then discuss how guests are met and how you greet them, and offer some pointers on best practice.

'High quality is seldom achieved by chance. It is almost invariably the outcome of care, attention to detail, a fitness for the purpose intended, allied to a genuine concern for the needs, comfort and convenience of the user.'

Enquiry and arrival

- THE IMPORTANCE OF ENQUIRIES

- DEALING WITH ENQUIRIES

THE IMPORTANCE OF ENQUIRIES

A guest's first impression of your B&B will, on many occasions, be by telephone. They may phone to find out about the accommodation and availability, or even to make a booking. This is a crucial point in the guest's journey, as it is at this point that they decide either to make a reservation or to try somewhere else.

It may seem like stating the obvious to talk about how to answer a telephone, but, as the owner of the B&B, your will need to answer the following questions. Who is answering the telephone? It may not always be you. Will that person know what information to give? Will they know what information to ask for? How will they answer? Will the phone be switched on to the answer machine or diverted to a mobile when you are out?

DEALING WITH ENQUIRIES

Do you normally answer your telephone with your name, the name of your house, your telephone number, or just by saying 'hello'? How will the caller react to these separate greetings? Is it more reassuring to hear 'Rosewood B&B' or a telephone number? If you do answer with your telephone number, then the caller will want to establish whether they have reached the right place. By answering with the name of your B&B, you will automatically let the caller know that they have dialled the right number.

It is a good idea to keep your booking diary and personal diary close to your main phone (you may, of course, have more than one). Make sure that this phone is as accessible from all parts of the house as possible. You need to bear in mind that enquiries can come at all times of the day and night, and you could be in the middle of cleaning the rooms or serving breakfast when an enquiry is made.

The caller may want to know only what you have to offer, or whether you have rooms available for certain dates, or they may just want to ask for a brochure. It is a very good idea to have a checklist by your phone. This can include all the relevant questions to ask, and can be used by any member of the family answering the telephone. The most important pieces of information are going to be the caller's name, their contact phone number, and, of course, the dates they are after and the type of room they have requested. You might also want to ask for a home address.

After a time, handling enquiries will become automatic for you, but it may not be so easy if others answer the phone. For all enquiries, it is well worth keeping that checklist by the telephone, with information on the rooms and key points to tell the caller, such as the type of rooms you offer, whether they are ground floor, whether they have a view, and any policies you may have regarding smoking, children or minimum ages – and then, of course, your prices. If you have a website, you can also mention this to the caller for further information, especially if the site contains photographs that you know help to sell your accommodation.

CONVERTING ENQUIRIES INTO BOOKINGS

Some telephone calls may initially be just enquiries on availability and prices. It is not unusual for someone to call a number of B&Bs to compare prices and find the best deal. This does not necessarily mean they are trying to find the cheapest place to stay, and you should always consider an enquiry as a potential booking.

To convert an enquiry into a sale, always emphasise any plus points. Never exaggerate, but advise the caller of any special features or added convenience – for example, if there is off-road parking, a quiet room overlooking the garden, or an en suite ground-floor room with its own entrance. Whatever the feature is, it may be worth mentioning it. Do not underestimate an everyday feature that you may take for granted.

RESPONDING TO ENQUIRIES

For all enquiries, consider how you record the caller's details. Rather than writing them down on the back of a scrap of paper, which may easily get lost, think about having a diary, an enquiry book or a standard form, kept by the telephone, which you can easily complete with their details and any special requests. You can head the columns 'name', 'address', 'contact telephone number', and so on, as appropriate.

Record any indication of dates that the caller may give, as well, and send them your brochure immediately – callers may often contact a number of other B&Bs as well. You could even include with the brochure some relevant local information, such as leaflets on local attractions, or a 'what's on' guide. This shows extra care and attention and is the kind of thing that could help convince them to book your accommodation, but you may want to be careful that the leaflets do not take the postage costs above that of a first class stamp! You may also receive enquiries by letter and email. These should also receive immediate attention.

WHAT IF YOU ARE OUT? DIVERTING CALLS AND

ANSWER MACHINES

Although you are running a business from home, there will be times when you are not available to answer the telephone. You may be out seeing people, or running errands, or you may just be out for a walk when the phone rings.

For such occasions, you may want to think about transferring incoming calls to a mobile telephone, so that you can always take the call. If you do this, you need to remember that it may not be so convenient to take details or to give information if you are in the supermarket, at the bank or walking the dog. But you can keep a notepad on you at all times, take callers' details and call them back as soon as you are home. Some B&B owners keep a small booking diary on them at all times, so they can instantly advise callers whether they have rooms available or not. At the very least, you may want to take the caller's telephone number and promise to call them later that day.

If it is going to be a problem diverting calls, an answer machine would be a perfectly acceptable alternative, although you need to make sure that you respond to enquiries as soon as possible. Record a message that asks the caller to leave their name and number, and says that you will get back to them as soon as you can. And don't forget to use the B&B name as confirmation that the caller has the right location.

Bookings

You should plan to have a simple system for dealing with all bookings efficiently and effectively. This will ensure that you have the correct information, and that your guests know exactly what the room rate includes, and any other relevant information, such as your policy on smoking. Once you have made a booking, you have entered into a contract. Make sure that customers understand your policies. Having a simple system should help to avoid any confusion such as over-booking and missed reservations, and it can record any special requests, such as a late or early arrival.

A useful tool for a simple booking system is a large-format diary with ruled-off sections for each room. A system of this sort is a useful way of recording guests' details.

INFORMATION TO ASK FOR

You do not want to sound too officious when taking a booking, but it is important to get the necessary information from the caller. What time are they expecting to arrive? It would not produce a good impression if a guest arrived while you were in the middle of the school run or out shopping, and no one is at home. Alternatively, they may be planning to arrive late at night, perhaps after attending a concert, and you do not want to have re-sold the room, having assumed that they were not coming.

It could be useful to say something along the lines of 'You are welcome to arrive anytime from four o'clock until (whatever time is suitable for you and your family)'. It is worth asking for a contact telephone number and, as most people have mobiles these days, it can prove very helpful if they have not arrived after the time advised.

You need to know whether your guests have any special requirements, and whether they know how to find you. These two questions are very useful in anticipating the needs of the guest. The definition of quality at the start of this chapter included the words '*a genuine concern for the needs of the user*'. Anticipation of guests' needs includes pre-empting their questions with the offer of information. It can be inconvenient, for you and for them, if a guest forgets to ask for something and has to call back. You will be offering a better service if you are able to provide all relevant information at the time of booking.

Most guests will volunteer any information on special requirements, such as a vegetarian diet, or conditions, such as mobility problems, but make sure there is a 'special requirements' question on your checklist.

Enquiry and arrival

- THE IMPORTANCE OF ENQUIRIES

- DEALING WITH ENQUIRIES

Bookings

- INFORMATION TO ASK FOR

- DEPOSITS

- RESPONSE TO BOOKINGS

- PASSING TRADE

DEPOSITS

A booking that does not show up loses the B&B money, and many B&Bs have a cancellation policy to protect them against the this happening. Another protection is to request a deposit, which is a common but not universal practice – you can legally retain a deposit if a booking is cancelled. Make the caller aware of any cancellation policy at the time of booking or, if you confirm the booking, after receipt of the deposit. Consider what the terms of the cancellation policy will be. It is not unusual to request the first night's charge or a nominal amount – say, £20 – upfront. But you must be clear at what point the guest forfeits their deposit. It could be 24 hours in advance, if you are in a busy location where you are likely to get another booking, or three days if you are in a very quiet location.

RESPONSE TO BOOKINGS

It is always prudent to follow up a telephone or email booking with written confirmation. By doing this, you are reassuring the visitor of your commitment to providing their accommodation, and ensuring that there have been no mistakes in taking the booking. You can mention any cancellation policy in the confirmation; some B&Bs in very busy locations even suggest that guests consider taking out holiday cancellation insurance in case they should need to cancel. This may be appropriate in a coastal resort, where a booking can sometimes be for a week or longer.

Finally, find out where the guest is coming from and how easy it will be for them to find you. Some guests manage very well from a short briefing on the phone, or you could mention that your brochure includes directions. Some B&Bs print a route from the guest's home location to the B&B using a route-planning website. Alternatively, you could send a copied sketch map showing your location, with directions.

Be prepared to respond in different ways to different guests. You could even send details of any special events that are happening in the area during their stay, or information about places of interest – if you did not do this with their initial enquiry. It is not uncommon for guests, when they are uncertain about their plans, to book one night without committing themselves to additional nights. A well-handled booking and warm welcome can turn a one-night booking into a three-night stay, or encourage repeat stays and recommendations to friends and family.

PASSING TRADE

Depending on your location, you may be able to pick up passing trade as well as pre-booked accommodation. You may have a bold vacancy sign on display, and list facilities to entice guests to stay. Alternatively, you may only want pre-bookings, and have no exterior signage at all.

It is especially important, if you are happy to accept casual callers looking for accommodation, to keep your rooms ready and freshly aired. Guests will often want to view the rooms before making a decision to stay. Always having rooms ready could mean the difference between getting a booking or not.

First impressions on arrival

You never have a second chance to make a first impression. Those impressions are vital in starting the guest off on the right footing, and ensuring that they are happy with their stay. A poor first impression can often result in a guest finding fault with other aspects of their stay. Very often, a complaint about a stay in a B&B is based on a poor first impression, after which all else seemed to go wrong.

For some guests, the first impression may start with the telephone enquiry; if not, it will start on arrival. Whether you are on a busy high street or seafront esplanade, or tucked away in a rural location, you want guests to arrive in a pleasant frame of mind. You may suggest that this is out of your control, but it does start with a guest finding your B&B easily.

SIGNAGE

Not all B&Bs have signs to advertise themselves, but you should have something that identifies you as the B&B that the guests are booked into. Any signage that you have, even if it is just a house name, needs to be clear and well lit. You may want your signage to stand out, particularly if you are competing with other properties in the street or in the same area. But, if you do not want casual callers checking to see whether you have rooms available late at night, think about having a removable sign, a 'No Vacancies' insert, or the ability to switch off illumination.

Finding your B&B may be relatively straightforward for guests arriving in daylight, and the directions you provided may help. But what if they are arriving after dark and in the rain? If your B&B is one of those that have no prominent signage – perhaps because you want to maintain a low profile and not upset the neighbours – make sure you have an easily visible house nameplate, or an unusual feature (such as a white-painted milk churn at a farmhouse B&B) to identify the entrance. One of the easiest signs to spot can be that of your quality assurance rating.

A final point to be aware of is that some signs require planning permission.

LIGHTING

Is there sufficient lighting around your B&B for guests when they arrive? You could use sensor lighting to highlight the front door, parking areas, and the route from their car to your entrance door, but you need to think carefully about where you site it. It needs to be effective for guests when arriving and unloading their cars, and perhaps to illuminate the boot. It may also need to be on quite a long time: guests will often take longer to unload their car than you will to unload the shopping.

PARKING

Will it be immediately obvious where guests can park their car, assuming, that is, you have parking space? You may not want to change the character of your home, but it may nevertheless be worth considering a small but clear sign indicating 'guest parking'.

Convenient parking is an important consideration for many guests. If guests have to park on the roadside, check out where they have parked, so that their vehicle does not inconvenience your neighbours. If your B&B is on a farm, or if another business operates from your home, you may need to make it evident where guests should park to avoid other traffic.

DO GUESTS KNOW WHERE TO GO NEXT?

Once guests have parked their car, will it be obvious which is the door they should go to? At some properties the front door is by no means obvious. You may have a property with two entrance doors, one of which is blocked up and no longer used, while the main entrance used is the former kitchen door. This may be obvious to you, but will it be to the guest arriving for the very first time?

You can use planters, hanging baskets and lighting to good effect to frame the front door and make it obvious from a distance. You run a B&B not a hotel, so you do not need a sign that says 'entrance', but you do need to make the entrance obvious.

GARDENS

It obviously helps to keep gardens or grounds neat and tidy, if you have them. Year-round external maintenance is important. Lots of weeds and unkempt bushes, or broken gutters and damaged external decoration, will not help to create that positive first impression. Even if you have little by way of a garden or no garden at all, then you can still introduce colour with hanging baskets, or wall-fixed planters, both of which will add character to the property.

ENTRANCE

Is there a working doorbell for the guests when they arrive? Are you there to meet them? Is the hall light on?

Meeting and greeting your guests should not be difficult – one of the pleasures of running a B&B is meeting many interesting people. Remember that guests who have driven a long way are likely to want to unwind. They will expect to be shown to their rooms, but help with their luggage, or the offer of a cup of tea, will be warmly welcomed.

What arrangements will you make for the time when you cannot be there to meet your guests? Emergencies do crop up, and it is always useful to have a contingency plan (leaving a key under the mat with a note on the front door is definitely not the best method). If you can organise a friend to meet and greet them, and show them to their rooms, this will obviously be a more acceptable arrangement than for them to sit in the car or stand on the doorstep until you get back.

As they step into your home, they will take in the ambience of your property. Are the lights on, and is the entrance hall tidy? Could you place a vase of fresh flowers in the hallway? The appearance and smell of fresh flowers can instantly set a welcoming tone on arrival.

It is often useful to point out the breakfast room, the lounge (if there is one) and any other areas guests may use when you are taking them to their rooms.

PREPARING THE ROOMS

When you are preparing a room, using a checklist ensures that you do not overlook anything. Check for blown light bulbs and missing room information folders, reset any bedside clocks and ensure their alarm is turned off. Even check for a badly tuned TV. Such small points will perhaps only be noticed when they are not attended to.

If you have guests who are arriving after dark or on a cold winter evening, think about how much more pleasant it would be if you showed them into a room with the curtains drawn, and bedside lights and the heating on. Preparing the bedrooms for guests can make a very strong first impression and, as the quality definition states, illustrates 'attention to detail and care for guests'. A little touch like this goes a long way.

REGISTERING YOUR GUESTS

Your welcome routine, which involves showing guests to their rooms and pointing out facilities on the way, should also involve asking guests to register.

It is a legal requirement to keep a register of your guests, and you need to keep the register for at least 12 months. However, arriving in a B&B is not like arriving in a hotel, where you may have to complete forms before you get to your room. B&Bs, by their very nature, offer a more homely atmosphere.

You could keep a guest book and mark off columns with name, nationality and passport details (where applicable). Keep a booking diary in which you record this information. Some B&Bs use a registration form like the one below.

Guest Registration Form

Name

Address

Date

How did you find out about us?

Nationality

Passport number*

Next destination*

You should ask everyone their name and nationality unless you already have recorded these in your booking diary by the time the guest arrives. You need ask only non-Commonwealth citizens the questions marked on the form with an asterisk. But the really useful question to ask is the question in bold – How did you find out about us? You may have asked this question at the time of taking the booking, or verbally on arrival, but having a record of the answers can prove especially useful when you are deciding how to advertise your B&B. If you have this question on the form, it becomes a marketing tool, helping you track what adverts or websites are working for you, how much business comes from the TIC, how many bookings were referred by other B&Bs or recommended by previous guests, and whether leaving your business cards in local shops has worked or not. We will look at growing your business in more detail in Chapter 8 but, for now, consider tracking how guests found your details.

ENHANCING THE WELCOME

Guests who have travelled a long way to stay with you may appreciate a cup of tea and use of the lavatory as soon as they arrive. Show them to their room and briefly advise them on anything that may be crucial to their comfort, such as how to use the shower controls and which key opens the front door. You can include any other information in a room folder. Depending on the kind of B&B you run, you may consider offering them tea in the guests' lounge. If they take up the offer, they will then be able to complete their registration, in the guest book or on a form, in comfort. Alternatively, you could leave the form in their room and ask them to complete it later.

With leisure guests, offering a pot of tea or a cold drink can provide an opportunity to supply advice on the local area. It is also a good opportunity to suggest somewhere for dinner. However, after an initial 'opener', the best thing may be to offer to help with any information, telling your visitors to 'just ask'.

If you do not have a guest lounge, you can still offer to provide fresh milk for the room tea tray. Offering an additional service shows additional care and attention, and can help enhance first impressions. But be careful: read your guest's body language. If you feel they want to be left alone, try not to fuss over them. Advising on this aspect of your hospitality is difficult, since the host's personality can add to (or sometimes detract from) the overall quality of the stay. The best advice is to be yourself.

ASKING ABOUT BREAKFAST

You need to think about how you find out what your guests want for breakfast. From your point of view, depending on the style of your breakfast and what you offer, it may be important to have an early indication of what they want, especially if you will be cooking it to order. But, then, it is not ideal to hand out a breakfast menu the moment a guest steps inside your front door, especially if they are planning to go out for an evening meal, when the last thing on their mind will be breakfast.

There are no hard-and-fast rules about this. You have to consider what is practical for you, but balance this with what is most convenient for the customer. If you need to know your guests' requirements beforehand, think about using a breakfast order form. You would not need to print this specially; it could be just a normal breakfast menu printed from a PC with tick boxes against each item, and a place for them to give the time they would like breakfast served. You could leave this form in their room, and ask guests to fill it in when they are ready and to leave it on the hall table, or somewhere convenient, before a set time that night.

Guests will have different requirements for breakfast, and will spend differing amounts of time over it. Some guests will not want to linger over breakfast – a business traveller, for example, is more likely to want their breakfast and then depart without delay. Conversely, a guest on a break may be happy to order at leisure and take time reading the morning paper, as breakfast is being cooked. Either way, advance notice can help you to have breakfast prepared at the time guests required it. Bear in mind that all the guests might choose to eat at the same time – but at least you will be ready!

DINNER

Occasionally guests may request dinner. A number of B&Bs do offer dinner, for various reasons: for some, it is because their guests expect it (it is a traditional part of the stay at some coastal resort B&Bs, for example); at others, it is to meet the specific needs of some guests (sometimes a single female business traveller might prefer not to eat in the local pub, but to have a meal in the comfort of the B&B, for example); or the

First impressions on arrival

- SIGNAGE
- LIGHTING
- PARKING
- DO GUESTS KNOW WHERE TO GO NEXT?
- GARDENS
- ENTRANCE
- PREPARING THE ROOMS
- REGISTERING YOUR GUESTS
- ENHANCING THE WELCOME
- ASKING ABOUT BREAKFAST
- DINNER

Case Study
Dinner or No Dinner?

This question arouses considerable debate among people who run B&Bs, and the answer is usually 'No'. However, not everyone is as categorical as this; some people who serve dinner say 'Well, we do if we really have to, but we would rather not', while others are cheerfully willing to do so if they know that they are meeting their market's demand by doing so.

A typical case of the latter is a seaside resort B&B/small guesthouse. It is interesting to note their answers to the following questions:

What percentage of your guests have dinner?

We are open all year and the pattern varies. In June/July/August about 90% to 100% of guests have dinner; in the winter this figure can drop to about 25%, but this can go up when bowls players and other special interest groups are in town. We always ask our bookings; 'knockers' (chance customers) only usually want B&B, but we can fit the odd extras in.

What time do you serve? Always early, at five thirty so that guests can make the shows in season. That way we are free from about seven o'clock.

What is the choice and what do you charge? We always offer fruit juice, followed by soup; then always a roast, or salad with meat (or an alternative to that) or a vegetarian dish; a hot dessert or ice cream, followed by cheese and biscuits if guests want it, and tea or coffee. We decide what's provided but we will try to meet reasonable demands – one man asked for sausages all week! There is an extra £6.00 on top of the B&B charge.

Is it profitable? No, not really!

Why do you do it? It goes with the territory. It's not only fitting in with the shows, even though that's an important part of it. Quite a lot of our customers are

continued

older and they do not want the bother of going out in the scrum for their evening meal. It definitely keeps our occupancy up as well, as the service meets the expectations of a lot of our main market.

So it is worth it? Oh yes! I know that it's appreciated from the comments and cards, but the added bonus is in the repeat business.

First impressions
on arrival

- SIGNAGE
- LIGHTING
- PARKING
- DO GUESTS KNOW WHERE TO GO NEXT?
- GARDENS
- ENTRANCE
- PREPARING THE ROOMS
- REGISTERING YOUR GUESTS
- ENHANCING THE WELCOME
- ASKING ABOUT BREAKFAST
- DINNER

owners may simply enjoy cooking, and offer dinner happily to all guests.

You do not have to offer dinner. Even though it can create good will, it can be a labour-intensive activity for little financial reward, and the price you can charge may not make up for the cost of ingredients, the time taken to prepare and cook the meal, and the washing up afterwards. Offering an evening meal to all guests may raise their expectations of what you will provide, but reacting to a request from a single female guest or an elderly couple may simply be seen as an extension of your hospitality. And, in this respect, simply extending the family meal to provide an additional portion for one guest is not too onerous.

If you do offer dinner and promote it in your advertising, do not assume you must offer a wide range of choices. You are not operating a restaurant; guests will not have the same expectations from your B&B as they would from a restaurant. It is quite acceptable to offer a set dinner, and for it to be homely in style and content.

How much you charge for dinner will be up to you and will depend on what you want to offer your guests, but charging a reasonable amount to cover the cost of ingredients and your time should be acceptable. Pointing guests in the direction of good local alternatives will meet the needs of the majority of customers. If you have only recently started up your B&B, you may be best advised to defer a decision on dinner, and see what the demand is like in your first six months or year of operation.

Next steps

In the next chapter we continue the guest's journey with their accommodation. We will start by looking at the bedrooms, and then the bathroom, analysing what makes a stay comfortable and what little touches you can add to enhance the guest's stay and make it more memorable.

Chapter 6
The stay

This chapter starts by looking at how to
ensure that your bedrooms are comfortable
for your guests. The definition of quality has
the words '*a fitness for the purpose intended
allied to a genuine concern for the needs,
comfort and convenience of the user*'. There
are suggestions on how to create a room that
will suit the needs of different guests but
remain homely and comfortable to stay in.
Towards the end of the chapter we look at the
bathrooms and factors you should consider
for making them easy to use. And we finish
by looking at one of the most important
areas for guests – cleanliness – and how
attention to detail can make the difference
between a good stay and an excellent stay.

Space

The amount of free space available after furnishing and
equipping the room will affect a guest's comfort. If you have
used the scale drawings, as suggested in Chapter 2, you may
already have a good idea of the shape of your guest rooms
and what they will accommodate. How comfortably did the
furniture fit when you placed it in the room?

As you plan the furnishing of your rooms, bear in mind the
height of ceilings, especially any sloping ceilings. Alcoves
may not be able to take free-standing furniture, but built-in
units could be a suitable way of using the space.

Remember, too, that visitors need storage space, not only for clothing, but also for cases and bags. If a room is crammed full and there is no suitable area for luggage, guests may end up using other furniture, such as the top of a wardrobe, which will be less easy to reach. If they have to use a chair for storage, that will compromise their comfort; if they are a single guest in a twin-bedded room and can find nowhere to store their things, they may use the spare bed, which may end up spoiling your bedcover.

How easily will guests be able to get in and out of bed? If you have squeezed a double bed into a room that really has space only for a single bed, can both guests get in and out of bed without having to climb over one another? Placing double beds up against walls may be acceptable for friends stopping over, but guests in a B&B will view it less favourably. You might consider placing twin beds against the wall with a gap in between, but avoid placing them side by side – this puts guests who want to sleep in separate beds very close together, which may itself be inconvenient.

Can the guest open and close all drawers and wardrobe doors? It is frustrating for guests if the wardrobe has been placed so close to the bed that they cannot easily open it, or they cannot open windows because there is furniture in the way. If something cannot be used for the purpose intended, then it is not the best quality.

You should also consider how essential items fit into the room. To meet the minimum standards for the NQAS, every bedroom should have a chair. But can you fit a chair in when all other items of furniture have been placed in the room?

In the rest of this chapter we will consider alternatives to some items of furniture that can help open a room up and allow it to be used easily, while still providing the essentials.

Beds

You have different needs when buying a bed for a commercial establishment catering to a succession of different guests from the needs of a homeowner buying a bed for personal use in a domestic situation.

If an uncomfortable bed or poor quality bedding prevents guests from sleeping, they will remember their stay for the wrong reasons, which is likely to affect repeat and referral business. Guests spend the main part of their stay in bed, and the beds should be of a suitable quality to offer greater durability for you, and optimum comfort for the guest.

The composition of a bed is quite complex. It may have an interior sprung mattress, which may be open coil, continuous springs or pocket springs. A non-sprung mattress might be latex, foam or fibre. However, the mattress is only half the story. The base of the bed is equally vital, and it is important to remember that a mattress and a base work together to provide support and comfort. The base can be boarded and firm, sprung, slatted, or a mesh base. Some models also provide storage.

When buying a bed, you should always consider the mattress and base as a pair and ensure that they are designed to go together.

The National Bed Federation and the website www.sleep council.com (01756 791089) are able to offer help and guidance in the choice and care of beds.

WHICH SIZE OF BED SHOULD YOU HAVE?

Beds used to come in standard sizes of a double (4ft 6in) and a single (3ft), but now queen-sized and king-sized doubles, and wider singles are becoming more common. Zip-and-link beds (two single beds that can be zipped together into a large double) are also popular and provide you with greater flexibility in the usage of your rooms. If you choose zip-and-link, the singles can be either 2ft 6in or 3ft. It is doubtful that a 2ft 6in bed will meet the expectations of two large adult guests if the room is sold to them as a twin. This may not cause a complaint, but will cause a disappointment. Bear in mind that the larger beds will also require non-standard-sized linen, and may require more effort when doing the laundry.

Space

Beds

- WHICH SIZE OF BED SHOULD YOU HAVE?

- SHOULD THE BED HAVE A HEADBOARD?

- WHAT TYPE OF BEDDING AND PILLOWS SHOULD YOU USE?

- GUESTS' ALLERGIES

- DUVETS OR BLANKETS?

- TOP SHEET, OR NO TOP SHEET?

- SPARE BLANKETS

- GENERAL DECOR OF THE ROOMS

SHOULD THE BED HAVE A HEADBOARD?

You will need to have a headboard (not all beds have one fitted), not only for the guest's comfort but also to protect your walls. Headboards prevent the bed from moving away from the wall if the guest sits up in bed, and will stop the pillow from falling down the back of the bed. What type of headboard will be most suitable? A wooden or brass frame headboard may suit the bed frame, but a padded board may be more comfortable. Consider also that if you purchase a fabric-covered headboard it may get marked and need more maintenance.

WHAT TYPE OF BEDDING AND PILLOWS SHOULD YOU USE?

Cover mattresses and pillows in protectors, which keep them in better condition and extend their life. If you accept young children, you may also need to use waterproof mattress protectors. Not all guests will appreciate these, however, as they prevent the body from 'breathing' properly, and usually make guests sweat, especially in hotter weather, making for a very uncomfortable night's sleep. If you feel you must use a plastic mattress protector, why not put additional padding between it and the bottom sheet, to enhance comfort. It is good practice to use a plastic protector only on a bed for young children, but, again, it will be a matter of the guests' expectations. Do you have a waterproof protector on your own bed? Plastic or rubber mattress protectors are not acceptable for adults in NQAS.

GUESTS' ALLERGIES

Guests with allergies may not thank you for providing down duvets and feather pillows, so it may be worthwhile also having synthetic, non-allergenic duvets and pillows available. Most guests will tell you in advance if they have this type of special requirement.

DUVETS OR BLANKETS?

The majority of people in their own homes and B&Bs use duvets, which are now more popular than blankets. Think about the filling when selecting a duvet, either man-made fibre, or down; the best quality down duvets can provide warmth in the winter and yet remain cooler in the summer, but synthetic duvets may be easier to maintain and clean.

You need to think about the tog rating, too. Guests will find it hard to sleep under a 13-tog rated duvet in the middle of a hot summer. Split-tog-rated duvets can be excellent, and can offer greater flexibility for you and your guests, but you will need extra space to store them.

If you plan to use sheets and blankets – and there are many B&Bs that do – there are certain points you need to consider. Bed sheets vary widely in quality. They may be made of natural fibres, man-made fibres, or a mixture of the two. Cotton sheets come in varying degrees of quality, with Egyptian cotton often regarded as the best quality. Polyester/cotton mixes will be less expensive and may be easier to wash, dry and iron, but they are prone to pilling. As far as colours are concerned, you might want to use white linen throughout, as it is interchangeable. Or you may decide to have co-ordinated colours for each room to tie in with the decoration (many B&Bs refer to their rooms by colour – the blue room, the pink room, etc.).

TOP SHEET, OR NO TOP SHEET?

Whether to have a top sheet with a duvet is quite a widely debated point with B&B operators. Ultimately it will be for you to decide, but it is worth considering some guest perceptions first. Some B&B operators provide a freshly laundered top sheet under their freshly laundered duvets as an extra consideration for their guests. This can be especially welcome in very hot weather, when the guest has the option of removing the duvet while still having the sheet to provide light cover.

With bed usage in their own homes, people with duvets usually sleep directly under the duvet, on top of a bottom sheet, as you may do. One of the country's leading travel accommodation chains provides that same arrangement, as it mirrors consumer use and familiarity. Of course, there are other operational reasons for the arrangement.

Some B&B operators provide top sheets and duvets on their beds and, while changing the sheets for each new guest, treat the duvet and its cover in the same way as blankets (not changing the duvet cover at the same time

Beds

- WHICH SIZE OF BED SHOULD YOU HAVE?
- SHOULD THE BED HAVE A HEADBOARD?
- WHAT TYPE OF BEDDING AND PILLOWS SHOULD YOU USE?
- GUESTS' ALLERGIES
- DUVETS OR BLANKETS?
- TOP SHEET, OR NO TOP SHEET?
- SPARE BLANKETS
- GENERAL DECOR OF THE ROOMS

as the sheets). The disadvantages in this approach distinctly outweigh any operational convenience. The top sheet folds over blankets and the same can be done with the duvet, true. But blankets do not crease in the same way as cottons and poly-cottons. Anything less than perfect presentation will disappoint customers.

People do not usually sleep with blankets directly next to the skin, either, which they are much more likely to do with your duvet – so the cover will hold the smell of perfumes, aftershaves and other bodily smells. Always launder the duvet cover for each new guest, ideally with perfect pressing.

SPARE BLANKETS

Spare blankets can be stored in the wardrobe for guests to use if they need them. They will look neater if they are placed in a zipped bag than if they are just left loose at the bottom of the wardrobe.

GENERAL DECOR OF THE ROOMS

You need to give some thought to how easy the walls will be to maintain, however you decide to decorate them. If you use wallpaper, bear in mind that there may be the occasional tear when luggage or furniture are moved. Keep some spare rolls to patch up damaged areas; it will be a lot easier than papering every twelve months. Walls that are painted should prove a lot easier to maintain, as you will only have to touch up scuff marks as they occur – but remember to buy more paint than you initially require.

As well as decorating the rooms, are there additional touches that can help lift the room's appearance, add interest and enhance the character of the accommodation? People often overlook the use of mirrors, which can have two main advantages for the guest: first, they can make a small room feel much bigger; and secondly, they add ease of use to a room, enabling guests to check their appearance before they leave for the day. Make sure you choose the right mirror: a dressing-table mirror may be fine for putting on make-up but not for checking your appearance from head to toe; a full-length mirror will improve ease of use for the guest. Think about where to put the mirror and make sure there is good lighting for it. Having the mirror on the back of a wardrobe door is of no use if the door can only be partially opened and, when open, lies in shadow.

Adding pictures of local scenes or original prints and paintings can all help lift a room, whereas leaving your child's poster on the wall will almost certainly impair its attractiveness.

Furniture

Customers expect a wardrobe or hanging area in their room, drawers, bedside tables or fixed shelves by the bed, a dressing table with mirror or desk, and a chair for each guest – and these are the minimum requirement of the NQAS for furniture.

HANGING SPACE

If space is very limited, you do not have to provide a full, free-standing wardrobe, but there should be enough hanging space for six coat-hangers per person. You can provide this in the form of a hanging rail across the corner of a room, which may not be ideal but will suffice. Adding a curtain would help screen the hanging rail and make it look better. Hanging rails that fix to the back of doors are also possible, although these need to allow space for free hanging. Simply hanging four items onto a hook is not suitable, as the clothes will become creased.

Consider also the range, usefulness and design of coat-hangers. Wire hangers should be removed, as they do not allow clothes to hang well. Shaped wooden hangers often offer the best design, and non-slip trouser hangers and padded hangers for blouses offer additional choice and convenience.

STORAGE SPACE

A bedside table containing drawers can sometimes prevent the need for additional chests of drawers, thereby saving space. If there is very little space beside the bed, consider fitting shelves instead of bedside tables. The smallest shelf would need to be about the area of a piece of A4 paper, suitable for a pair of glasses, a glass of water, and possibly a book.

You may have a dressing table with drawers, which can also avoid the need for a separate chest of drawers. If you do place a dressing table in the bedroom, consider how easy it to use. Can the guest sit at the 'table' comfortably, and is there a kneehole? A dressing table with a kneehole is much more comfortable to sit at than one without. Have you provided a suitable chair or stool? A dressing table with a mirror is easy to use, and one with a table lamp even easier.

How you furnish your rooms will in part depend on who will be staying at your B&B. Guests on holiday or on a weekend break will not normally need a writing surface but, should you have a lot of business people staying, you will need to provide somewhere for them to do some paperwork in the evenings. A dressing table may look nice, but will it be easy to work at? If you have a mix of guests, dual-use furniture – a dressing table that also serves as a work desk – can meet all needs well.

Many B&B owners find that there can be a shortage of storage space for their own belongings, and they end up having to use the guest bedrooms to store family clothing, bedspreads, and so on. Make sure that any wardrobes or cupboards containing your personal belongings are locked, out of use and out of sight. All you need to do for this is add a small lock to the cupboard doors, or at least tie a cord around the door handles of your wardrobe or cupboard, while leaving the guests' wardrobe free. You would then just need to tell the guest which is theirs wardrobe when you show them to their room.

If there is room, there are other pieces of furniture that will make the guest's stay even more comfortable: an extra small table may be useful; an armchair may offer much more comfort than a simple easy chair; a 'luggage rack' (this can be a chest at the base of the bed or a blanket box – it does not need to be the hotel style of rack) will provide somewhere to place bags.

Furniture
- HANGING SPACE
- STORAGE SPACE
Flooring
Window dressing

Flooring

Floors have to withstand a good deal of wear and tear, so it is important to choose material carefully. Laminate and stripped-wood flooring are currently very popular, and both these styles are easy to maintain. Carpeting helps to insulate and absorb noise, and comes in a wide range of quality and prices. If you are going to use carpets, do not neglect the underlay: the quality of underlay will make a large difference to the overall quality of a carpet.

Whatever style of flooring you decide on, always have it professionally fitted, making sure, for example, that the carpet is stretched and fitted correctly to the edges of the floor, and that laminates have no gaps between sections.

Window dressing

Window dressings need to be effective to exclude daylight and provide privacy. What level of blackout will the curtain provide? If a bedroom faces east, for example, will the early morning sun in midsummer wake the guest up at a very early hour? This is a relatively small point, but one that could make the difference between a good night's sleep and a restless one.

Curtains that are well lined always add to the overall appearance of the room. Curtains with interlining help further with insulation. Consider also if you are going to use tiebacks for the curtains. They often look better and hold the curtains away from the window, which allows more natural light into the room. Pelmets are another option.

Blinds are a popular alternative to curtains, or can be used in conjunction with them. They are especially useful in shielding the high late-afternoon sun in a south-west facing room in summer. Opt for the simpler designs, if possible: guests may not always find it easy to use blinds or curtains that are drawn by pull-cords.

Heating

You can heat rooms in many different ways, from warm air using floor ducts to electric radiators, storage radiators and, more commonly, central heating. But make sure that whatever form of heating you have is easy to use. If you have central heating, you can have radiators fitted with thermostat valves, which allow the guests to set the temperature to their tastes.

Air conditioning is not generally found in B&Bs, and would not be expected by a guest, although it would be helpful to provide a fan for those hot spells in the summer.

Lighting

Each bedroom should have practical lighting that is easy to control and effectively situated. There should be lights by each bed space, allowing guests to turn a light off easily when they go to bed and to turn a light on easily should they need to get up during the night. This means a light on each side of a double bed; with twin beds, the bedside light could be placed in between the beds, allowing each guest to reach it, but ideally the lights would be on the far side of each bed, so that each guest can switch their light on without disturbing the other.

You need also to think about where to put bedside lights to make it easy for guests to read in bed. A bedside lamp that is lower than the guest's head when they are sitting in bed will blind them every time they switch the light on. Try to have bedside lights that are a little above head height when the guest is sitting in bed – wall-mounted lights may be best for this, or you may have tall lamps that meet this need. Do not neglect the light controls. Will guests be able to reach the wall-light switches easily from bed, or will they have to get out of bed just to turn the lights off? Have you thought about having a dual switch for the main light, with a switch by the bed for ease of use?

Lighting will also be useful by dressing tables and mirrors. Overall, how much lighting you need will depend on the size and shape of your room, but try to ensure that all areas are illuminated and provide a choice of lighting levels. Guests can always switch a light off if they want a more subdued ambience – or you can fit dimmer switches, which give guests full control over light levels.

Low-energy light bulbs will save you money in the longer term and are worth considering, but test them first for lighting levels – good lighting is particularly important for visually impaired and hearing impaired guests.

Accessories

Before providing an abundant supply of accessories, think about the main requirements of your guests. They will expect a hospitality tray, although it is not a minimum requirement of the NQAS – you could provide a tea tray in the hallway, or drinks on request. However, a tea tray in the bedroom is much more convenient for the guest, who will be able to make drinks without leaving the privacy of their room.

THE TEA TRAY

The tea tray can contain simply a kettle, tea, coffee, sugar and long-life milk, but would this be the best quality for *your* B&B? You may want to add a teapot, a teacloth for drying a cup after use, a choice of teas, decaffeinated coffee, hot chocolate, other hot drinks, sweeteners, fresh milk, water, coasters, biscuits, fruit or even a slice of homemade cake. Some of these extras can be provided at relatively low cost – indeed, it may just be a case of topping up supplies from your own kitchen cupboard – but they can have a big impact on the guest's stay and create a little distinctiveness.

When putting the tea tray together, have in mind how easy it is for the guest to use. Is there a convenient power point close by? Having to plug the kettle into a point half-hidden behind a piece of furniture, or having the kettle on the floor while it is boiling, is inconvenient, difficult and dangerous. And is there a waste bin close by for tea bags? You don't want guests leaving a trail of tea bag drips across the carpet!

Providing fresh milk for the tray can be less easy, especially in summer. You do not want the milk to go off before the guest has used it. You could consider placing the milk in a small thermos jug or flask to keep it chilled. Alternatively, you might provide a small jug of fresh milk on arrival, and provide another in the morning. Or you could provide a mini-refrigerator in the room with fresh milk in it. One option adopted by a number of B&Bs is to place a small refrigerator with fresh milk in the hallway. They also stock the refrigerator with cold drinks and chocolates, with guests paying by means of an honesty box system. This is an option that can be very popular in rural areas, where guests may have been out walking and will welcome a snack when they return. It is also a possible source of extra revenue.

THE TELEVISION

What type of TV should you get? A very large TV may be difficult to watch, and may take up too much space; too small, and the TV will be less easy to see from a distance; free-standing, it may be easy to see when sitting in the chair, but less easy to see when in bed; but, if wall-mounted, the TV may be easy to see from one point in the room, but not from any other. When you are siting it, think of all the positions from which the TV may be watched.

A remote control will make things more comfortable for guests, and TVs with teletext can be very useful, particularly for hearing impaired guests, who can watch with the subtitles on. You may even consider providing a TV listings magazine.

Televisions with built-in video players or DVD players can also be useful, especially if you have long-term guests who may want to watch a film rather than the TV. If you are near a university or college, visiting lecturers or foreign students may need to use a video or DVD player for their studies. Having one available in the lounge is useful, but having one in the bedroom is even more convenient. It is now becoming more common to find satellite and digital channels in B&Bs.

ROOM INFORMATION FOLDER

You can use a room information folder to provide emergency advice, but also to give local and tourist information.

A folder with plastic inserts can contain your breakfast menu, details on any other facilities that are available, such as an iron and board, TV channels and how to operate the clock radio. You could also include information on the local area, such as pubs and restaurants, with a selection of sample menus.

A WELCOME CARD

A welcome card provides a personal touch that normally goes down well with guests. It can be a blank greeting card, and can even match the colour of decor in the room. Apart from welcoming the guest, it can also include useful information: for example, how to call for assistance in case of an emergency at night (you can have a small hand-bell on the landing for this purpose, as long as it would be audible in your room; or you could mark your room clearly so that guests know where to go for help). Providing this kind of information is essential, but you will not necessarily want to stick signs on walls or on the back of bedroom doors. A card is a low-key but homely way of providing this information.

The welcome card can also remind guests of other relevant information, such as whether water is softened and unsuitable for drinking, or of your smoking policy. The card can be laminated for extra durability.

Your card might look something like this:

Accessories

- THE TEA TRAY
- THE TELEVISION
- ROOM INFORMATION FOLDER
- A WELCOME CARD
- OTHER ACCESSORIES

A Most Warm Welcome To

The Beeches

We do hope that you will be comfortable during your stay with us, and that we have managed to think of everything that you will need to be so.

If you can think of anything else that we may be able to help you with – please ask!

* * *

You will find a hairdryer in the dressing table drawer and a hot-water bottle in the wardrobe, along with a freshly laundered extra blanket in case you feel the chill.

Please ring the bell on the hall table in the event of any emergency at night.

In consideration of other guests, we politely request that you do not smoke in the bedroom.

John and Mary

OTHER ACCESSORIES

Try not to leave any personal photographs in bedrooms: these can make the B&B too personal and leave visitors thinking they are occupying your own room. However, you could consider providing those little extras that make all the difference – those 'screaming subtleties' that are highly effective but inexpensive.

Here is a list of some of the things that B&Bs provide for their guests. Among these, there will be some you will like and want to adopt, and some you will decide are not for you. Remember that you do not need to provide everything!

- A waste bin for tea bags, wrappers and litter.
- Reading material – magazines, books and leaflets can all be helpful (but do weed out any dog-eared or very out-of-date publications).
- Books on the local area.
- Radio alarm clock – but remember to check the time and switch the alarm off if you have a new guest arriving.
- Pot pourri sachets for the wardrobe and drawers – to add a fresh fragrance and avoid mustiness.
- Lining paper in drawers – to prevent splinters catching clothes.
- Hairdryer and clothes brush.
- Shoe-cleaning kit – especially helpful if you have guests attending a wedding or other smart event.
- Sewing kit – consider pre-threading some needles.
- Spare blankets and hot water bottle.
- Stationery.
- Fresh fruit – but consider also providing a knife, plate and napkin.
- Plants or flowers – having something animate in a room can add to its overall ambience and appearance.
- A comment card – this can request any suggestions or comments and is a good way of monitoring feedback.
- For annexe bedrooms, where guests need to come from outside to the dining room, an umbrella would be welcome on wet days.
- A torch for the rural B&B with a pub a short walk away.

Case Study

The B&B Eating Out Guide

When we first started running our B&B, guests would often ask us where they could go to eat. To begin with, we would give them directions to a couple of smart restaurants and the local Chinese. Fairly early on we realised that by doing this we were assuming that the cost of the meal would not be an issue. At the same time, we realised that people had such varied preferences (this coincided with our first vegetarian) that we decided that we needed to provide our guests with better information.

In the entrance hall we set up a large wall map with our B&B in the centre. Radiating out from the hub, we drew spokes and fixed business cards from all the local restaurants and pubs. Along each of the spokes we indicated the distance it would take either to walk to (for a couple of the nearby ones) or to drive to from our house. On a table under the map we now keep a large folder with plastic inserts. We put a copy of the menu in the inserts, with prices and directions. As we had no first-hand knowledge of all the different places, we included a blank sheet where guests could write their comments. Some have been amusing and brief, while others have been so detailed that we suspected they were from the Michelin guide! This page has been invaluable in providing a constructive critique, and it gives the guests another viewpoint, which they seem to like. We make them aware of our 'eating out map' in the room information files.

Housekeeping

Making beds, dusting, vacuuming and washing may seem so much a part of everyday home care as not to pose a problem. But, for the paying guests coming to stay in your B&B, every facet of what they use must be perfectly presented in terms of cleanliness. When they enter the bedroom, they really want to feel that no other guest has stayed there. Although they will already have gained initial impressions of your property from the enquiry and booking procedures, their first genuine impressions will be when they arrive. Not only will they take into account the visual appearance, but their other senses will come into play, such as smell and touch. When guests are taken to their room you may think they will immediately be wowed by the four-poster bed, or the view from the window, or the decor. But, if they open a drawer and find a previous occupant's sock, or turn on the TV and notice thick white dust, the effect of any adornments that you have added will quickly be lost.

For all levels of cleaning it is important to have a routine. You will carry out a thorough clean for a new arrival, but it will be less vigorous while they are staying. You will also carry out regular deep cleaning and spring-cleaning periodically, so for each there needs to be a routine. This will be particularly important if you employ staff, and even more so if there are staff changes or if staff are employed seasonally.

CLEANING

To begin with at least, it is useful to have a checklist for each area that is cleaned. Although you will be vacuuming and dusting every day, window cleaning may be a weekly job, and turning the mattresses something you do every three months.

When cleaning your rooms, think about how the guest may use the room. They may be sitting in the armchair when watching TV, they may be sitting in bed when reading, and they will be using the wardrobe to hang their clothes. Their perspective on the room may be slightly different from your own when you are doing the cleaning. Remember that their eye-line may reveal the underside of the bed, the area around the edge of the skirting boards, and the often-missed wedge of dust behind the bedroom door when it is closed.

What cleaning supplies will you use? Domestic brands may be your choice, but commercial brands may be more economical and more effective; you may also want to consider your environmental policies when buying supplies, and select those that are less harmful to the environment.

'DUST MAGNETS' AND 'HIDDEN ZONES'

You will need to be particularly vigilant about those areas of the bedroom that act like magnets for dust. Lampshades will attract dust because of the air movement created by the hot light bulb. A TV screen generates static, which will draw dust towards it. Curtains are often prone to getting dusty because they are near windows.

'Hidden' areas of the room are those areas you don't normally see, such as below a bed, on top of a wardrobe and behind the bedroom door. These areas are often missed when you are vacuuming a room with the door open, so remember to close the door before finishing. It is useful to check these areas on a frequent basis.

CLEANING SCHEDULE

Some points that you may want to include on your housekeeping schedule include the following:

- Open windows and switch on lights – this has the added advantage of warning you of any blown bulbs.
- Collect together water glasses, cups from tea trays and anything that will need to be washed. Collect up any rubbish from the waste bin.
- Check all storage areas for any objects left by previous guests, including drawers and wardrobes and the hook on the back of the bedroom door.
- Ensure wardrobes still have enough hangers, and drawers are not missing any linings.
- Check under the bed.
- Strip beds and remove dirty linen, and check for staining on mattress and pillow protectors, duvet or blankets.
- Valances (if used) can frequently become stained with shoe polish by guests sitting on the bed when cleaning their shoes.
- Remake the beds, ensuring that duvet cover fasteners are all in place. Fasteners can get damaged during ironing and buttons can become unattached. If you use a laundry

for your linen, make sure that there are no tears or
tiny holes.
- Dust, clean, polish and wet clean, working systematically
around the room from high to low. Pay special attention to
tops of mirrors, picture frames, door tops, headboards,
down the backs and sides of any easy seating, TV,
bedside tables, pelmets, curtain tracks and light shades.
- Clean windows if necessary, and other glass surfaces.
- Replenish hospitality tray and other accessories, including
the information folder, if you have one.
- Check all bedside lights, clocks, radio and TV, curtain
hooks or blind pulls.
- Thoroughly vacuum the floor.

CLEANING A ROOM FOR GUESTS WHO ARE STAYING

For guests who are staying, a less rigorous clean is usually
required, although this will depend on how long they are
staying. Start by taking cups and glasses that need washing,
then empty rubbish. Fold up any belongings and leave them
on a chair or other surface, but do not put them into drawers.
Replace bedlinen where necessary, and remake the bed.
Dust and spot clean if necessary, and replenish the tea tray
and any other accessories. Check light bulbs, curtain pulls,
TV tuning, and then vacuum.

DEEP CLEANS

On a frequent basis you will need to do a deeper clean.
Kettles will need regular de-scaling; lampshades and the tops
of pelmets are great dust collectors; mattresses need to be
vacuumed, turned and flipped every three months. Duvets
and blankets, including any spare blankets, will need to be
dry-cleaned; curtains will need washing or dry-cleaning; net
curtains and voiles will need to be washed often. Carpets
may need to be shampooed, and furniture moved for
vacuuming.

If you employ a cleaner, it is a good idea to identify daily,
weekly, monthly, and quarterly cleaning schedules to cover
all the areas detailed above.

Bathrooms

Guests will not spend as much time in the bathroom as in the bedroom, but the bathroom remains a crucial part of their stay. The quality of the bathroom, the strength of the shower, the amount of space to manoeuvre in and the accessories provided will all contribute to their memories of their stay. Guests will often clearly remember the quality of the bed, the quality of the shower or bath, and the quality of the breakfast, often comparing them with that provided at home.

What, then, are the key aspects of the bathroom that make a guest's stay comfortable?

DECORATION

A fully tiled bathroom will usually be easier to maintain than one with painted or papered walls. Mirrors are important: a large mirror and a small shaving mirror are both helpful. Think about where to place mirrors: if the washbasin is on one side of the room and the mirror is on the other, then someone having a wet shave will be to-ing and fro-ing between the two.

Pictures can help lift the appearance of the bathroom, but they are often badly affected by damp conditions.

FLOORING

Getting the flooring right is not straightforward. Carpeting can be very comfortable and warm underfoot, and can be suitable in a domestic bathroom, but carpeting can become unhygienic with use, and is less easy to keep clean – indeed, with excessive damp it can quickly deteriorate. Flooring tiles are more expensive, and are often considered to be of higher quality, but they can be very cold underfoot; guests use the bathroom in bare feet, so comfort is important. Some B&Bs have under-floor heating beneath tiled floors, which can offer the best of both worlds. Vinyl flooring is another alternative, being easy to maintain and relatively inexpensive.

HEATING

There are a variety of options for heating in bathrooms. You may have central heating in the bathroom or an electric fan heater. A heated towel rail can be a real bonus during seasons when the central heating is not switched on, and can help create a comfortable temperature and warm towels.

AIR EXTRACTION

In all bathrooms, and especially in shared bathrooms – where there may be continual usage of the room over a period of time – an extractor fan will prove invaluable. Extractor fans help clear the mist after a shower or bath, reduce dust accumulation and help prevent all the associated problems of damp, such as mildew and mould.

LIGHTING

For safety reasons, there should never be a bare light bulb in a bathroom: enclosed lighting is a requirement. This lighting must be effective, however, so plan the position of your lights carefully. Clear lighting will be needed above the washbasin, for shaving, and recessed down-lighters can be good because they are glare-free. Waterproof recessed light fittings above a shower cubicle can also be helpful.

It is worth mentioning that many guests who wear glasses remove them when in the bathroom, which leaves their vision impaired. Higher lighting levels – or perhaps a choice of light levels – can therefore be useful.

BATH OR SHOWER?

Guests tend to divide broadly into those who like showers and those who like baths, but the range of fixtures you install in your bathroom is likely to be dictated by space. Can you install a shower as well as a bath, or just a shower? Showers tend not to use as much water as baths, and are usually easier for disabled guests; but baths can be more relaxing and are usually more suitable for children. Whatever you have or decide to install, it will be important to ensure that there is sufficient water pressure and ample hot water at the times when guests need it.

If you have space for a bath, you can usually install a shower above it. This should use up no more space, but you will need to check that the ceiling allows someone to stand comfortably under the shower head (this is unlikely to be the case with a sloping ceiling). A shower with an adjustable rail can be very useful, especially if a guest wants to avoid getting their hair wet.

Make sure that any shower you have is easy to use and does not cause sudden changes in water temperature. For baths that have a fixed shower attachment, it is worth considering a shower screen rather than a curtain. Curtains are easily replaced and a screen will require extra cleaning, but screens are usually more efficient in helping to keep the floor dry. A shower curtain can also tend to get wrapped around the user, making it less user-friendly. Also consider the positions of soap dishes at appropriate heights.

Grab-handles in baths and in shower cubicles will also be helpful to guests, especially if they have any difficulties moving – for example, if they have damaged a knee or are pregnant. For similar reasons, check how slippery the surfaces are – they should be non-slip if they are going to ensure guests' safety. If they are not, provide non-slip mats.

STORAGE

People often provide too little space for guests' belongings in a B&B bathroom. When the guest arrives, they will bring a wash-bag. Will they have somewhere to place things? There may be a small shelf for their toothpaste and toothbrush, but what about their deodorants, shaving foam, razor, hairbrush, flannel, and so on?

Providing sufficient shelf-space, hooks for clothes and rails for towels all ensure that the bathroom is easy to use. If the bathroom is a shared facility, then sufficient surfaces and storage are even more important.

You will need to make guests aware of the plumbing arrangements if your property is not connected to the mains sewage system, or has small-bore waste pipes. A card placed on the WC cistern or permanently fixed to the wall in a prominent place should help to prevent the expense of calling out a plumber.

TOWELLING

The quality of towelling can vary considerably in terms of absorbency, weight, texture, softness, and in how well it wears after numerous washes. Does it dry evenly, or do its patterned headers and applied patterns create differential shrinkage?

You also need to think about the range of towelling you provide. A hand towel and a bath towel for each person are enough, of course, but, depending on the type of guest you have staying and the type of guest you want to attract, you might also want to provide a bath sheet, face cloth and bathrobe. If guests are using a private or a shared bathroom, which they have to leave their room to get to, a bathrobe can be helpful. It is not something they are likely to bring with them, so it will be greatly appreciated. A useful tip if you do provide a robe is to hang it in the wardrobe, but carefully folded, so you can tell whether the guest has used it and it needs washing. For example, place sleeves into opposite pockets, or tie the waistband into a bow. You may wish to introduce an environmental policy for the laundering of towels for your long-stay guests.

Pay some thought to the colour of the towels. White towels are popular, but might white towels in a mainly white bathroom, with a white bathroom suite and white tiles, be difficult for a visually impaired guest to see? A pastel colour might have the double advantage of adding distinctiveness to the bathroom, and allowing visually impaired guests to make things out more clearly. It can also add character and interest to the room, whereas an all-white appearance can be stark.

You will also need to provide a bathmat. In an en suite or private bathroom one mat will suffice, but in a shared bathroom a different mat for each guest could be useful. Two options here are placing a pile of mats on a side table, or placing rolled up mats in a basket for guests to help themselves.

TOILETRIES

Most guests will bring a range of personal toiletries including perhaps their favourite brand of shampoo or shower gel. What should you provide? As a minimum, make sure each guest has fresh soap, not necessarily a fresh bar of soap (which could get quite expensive), but possibly liquid soap. There are some very high-quality liquid soaps and, importantly for the guest, each time they push the dispenser they get fresh soap. Importantly for you, liquid soap creates less mess on the basin than a bar of soap, and you just need to keep the bottle topped up to make it look fresh and new for each guest.

If you do provide a fresh bar of soap – normally of guest size, although larger if guests are staying for a week – make sure it looks good. If it is wrapped when you buy it, keep it wrapped and, for best presentation, make sure that it does not get wet before it is used.

Additional toiletries you could provide include shower gel, shampoo, conditioner, bath foam or salts, cotton wool, cotton buds, tissues and so on. Shampoo and shower gel sachets can be very difficult to open, especially if the guest is already in the shower and has wet hands, and there is often only a small amount in each sachet. Provide bath foam if you have a bath, but keep it topped up so that it appears fresh.

A small basket of 'in-case-you-forgot' items can be a good idea, if you think it is appropriate. This could contain a travel toothbrush and toothpaste, a disposable razor, tissues, cotton wool, cotton buds, emery boards, sewing kit and shower cap.

Remember to provide plenty of toilet paper, and of appropriate quality.

Many B&B owners, mindful of the environmental impact of washing towels every day, make a point of letting their guests know about their environmental policy and ask them to place towels that they want to be changed in the bath or shower tray, but to leave all other towels on the towel rail.

CLEANING

A checklist is useful for cleaning the bathrooms, as it is with other rooms. Certain cleaning jobs will need to be done daily; indeed, with splashing from showers and general usage, most areas will need some attention on a daily basis. You might decide to do other jobs, like de-scaling the showerhead and toilet bowl, on a weekly or monthly basis.

As with bedrooms, you may be happy with domestic cleaning supplies, but commercial brands may be more economical and effective – although you may also want to bear in mind your environmental policies when purchasing cleaning supplies.

Again, when cleaning the bathroom think about how the guest uses the room. Their eye-line will often be at low levels, when they are sitting down or lying in the bath. At these levels they will notice the underside of the washbasin, the U-bend of the waste pipe and the edges of the floor. As with the bedroom, remember to check behind the bathroom door, not just for that wedge of dust that can accumulate but also for splashes on the door itself.

The main 'dust magnet' in the bathroom will be the extractor fan. This pulls in dust and can look very unsightly if not cleaned regularly. If you are in a hard-water area, keep a careful eye on accumulation of limescale around taps, wastes and shower controls – or in any part of the shower tray or bath that contains sitting water.

CLEANING SCHEDULE

Here is a possible cleaning schedule for you to do on a daily basis.

Start by opening the window, if there is one, to ventilate the room. Working from high to low, clean all areas, including the extractor fan, shower, basin, toilet, walls, bath and floor. Remove dust from extractor and check carefully for mould or mildew on tiles and the shower curtain. You may need to replace the curtain on a regular basis. Check for hair in all plugholes and in the corners and edges of the shower, and the room generally.

Clean the bath and clean, de-scale and then finally dry and polish the glass shower screen. Clean the basin, checking for toothpaste, soap and make-up residue, and polish the taps. Clean and brush the toilet bowl with appropriate cleaner, especially under the rim; flush, disinfect and leave scented cleaner in the bowl. Clean the seat and lid, dry it and ensure the toilet brush is clean and replaced in container.

Empty the rubbish bin and replace toiletries, towelling, glasses and toilet rolls; tidy your guests' personal toiletries;

make sure that your environmental policy on towel replacement is prominently displayed. Wash the floor, wipe the door handle and give the room a final once-over check.

Doing such a thorough clean each day will become routine and relatively quick, but it's really worth giving cleanliness in the bathroom extra attention to detail.

Test your rooms

It may seem unnecessary to test your rooms – after all, you designed them, decorated them and equipped them, so you should be familiar with them. But you should spend a night in each bedroom and use the bathroom yourself, not just once but on an annual basis. This will be help you to assess whether the guests are likely to experience any intrusive noise, such as the central heating boiler, whether the bedside lights are at the right height, and whether the shower is easy to use. Even better, get friends or family to use the other rooms, so that you can hear whether plumbing from adjoining rooms or other noise is audible.

Sleeping in your own rooms helps you to carry out your own self-assessment and see just how easy is it for guests to use the facilities, and whether the bedroom is comfortable and convenient to use, without any restrictions. Can you, for example, open the wardrobe door and boil the kettle safely?

The key point here is that you will be 'testing' a product that you are charging for, as well as using part of your home. It is a good exercise to look at how everything is to be used. Start with the bed. Is there sufficient space by the side of the bed? Is the shared table between twin beds so small that there is only room for one teacup? Are there enough drawers to contain a reasonable amount of clothing, and are they deep enough? Can the chair be used by someone who needs to work at a desk, or by an older guest putting on their socks? Does it work for someone watching TV, or will it be used as a luggage rack, because there is nowhere else to place your bags? Does the dressing table have to double up as a desk and a place to keep the tea tray? Is the lighting of sufficient wattage? Is the carpet starting to wear in parts because it

Bathrooms
- DECORATION
- FLOORING
- HEATING
- AIR EXTRACTION
- LIGHTING
- BATH OR SHOWER?
- STORAGE
- TOWELLING
- TOILETRIES
- CLEANING
- CLEANING SCHEDULE

Test your rooms

lacks underlay? When did you last walk barefoot on it? When the curtains are drawn across the windows, do they meet or do they leave a gap? And do they give total blackout? Can the temperature of the heating be controlled independently? If so, is the thermostat accessible? If the guest wants to use the hairdryer, is there a mirror by a power point? Does the full-length mirror need to be re-positioned? Is the TV visible from only the bed or one chair?

You could carry out the same assessment in the bathroom. Are the controls in the shower easy to operate? Does the pressure alternate and affect the temperature? Is there a soap dish or suitable container on a shower wall? With a bath that has an integral shower, does the spray from the head stay within the bath, or will it flood the floor? Is there good light intensity by a mirror for shaving or applying make-up? And are there suitable surfaces for wash-bags and hooks for clothing? Is the extractor fan powerful enough to keep condensation down? Is there any supplementary heating such as a towel rail?

Carrying out this room-by-room 'ease of use' self-assessment can be an eye-opener and will highlight what might not be working well and where there are points that could be developed.

Next steps

In the next chapter we look at the next part of the guest's journey: the morning after their comfortable night's sleep. This chapter looks at the second 'B' in B&B – the breakfast – and then goes on to look at departure, and how to provide each guest with a positive lasting impression of their stay.

Chapter 7
Breakfast and departure

As the second 'B' in B&B, breakfast can often be the most memorable part of a guest's stay. It is usually their last experience, leaves them with a good feeling in the morning and it provides you with an opportunity to chat with them and offer advice on places to see and things to do. For guests on holiday, it also provides you with an opportunity to create a distinctive experience for them. In this chapter we will look at ways of making breakfast a little more distinctive.

Where should you serve breakfast?

Where should you serve breakfast?

- HOW MANY TABLES?

- CROCKERY, CUTLERY, TABLEWARE

Whether you decide to serve breakfast in a breakfast room, a dining room, a lounge/diner or a large farmhouse kitchen, you will want to create an area that is comfortable and conducive to serving food. If you are using an extension to your kitchen such as a conservatory, and are 'on show', take extra care to present the kitchen in neat and tidy fashion for the guest. The kitchen can be a refuge for anyone running a B&B but, when it is visible, it will affect the overall impression of breakfast.

Wherever you decide to serve breakfast, you will need to think about the decoration and furniture of the room, and about whether other decorations (such as flowers or plants) may enhance appearances.

HOW MANY TABLES?
If you are able to use a dining room, how will you arrange the table? You may want to use a large table for all guests, or smaller tables that will seat two or four guests. Both have advantages. A larger table can generate more conversation

among guests, but it may be inconvenient for reaching things, and guests may find themselves having to pass the butter, sauces and cereals. To enable guests at each end of the table to reach everything they need it is not a bad idea to have doubling condiment points.

You may find individual tables easier to use when serving, as there may be more space for individual tea and coffee pots, toast racks and condiments. Where will guests sit? If you have a single guest facing a window but with their back to the rest of the room, it can restrict conversation with other guests and they could feel slightly uncomfortable.

A side-table can make service easier and allow you to provide a buffet-style breakfast. It is also a good way to display cold items for guests to help themselves to, such as juices, cereals, fresh fruit, compote and yoghurts.

CROCKERY, CUTLERY, TABLEWARE

Crockery, cutlery and dishes will need to be appropriate, durable and possibly dishwasher-proof. All crockery and cutlery should be matching and in good condition. Remove any crockery that is chipped. As well as main plates, you will need to provide side-plates, cereal bowls, cups or mugs and serving dishes. A uniform design could be helpful if anything gets damaged and needs replacing and also creates a high standard of presentation, making a good first impression on guests as soon as they enter the dining room.

Tablecloths and napkins, particularly when these are linen, lead to extra laundry costs. If your tables are of good quality wood, you may decide you do not need tablecloths. The laundry costs of linen napkins may prompt you to use paper napkins but keep the quality high, whatever you decide to use: a segment of kitchen roll does not serve the purpose well. A two-ply or three-ply napkin, possibly patterned, can be effective and can match the general colour theme of your dining room or crockery. Beware single-ply serviettes: they tend to tear very easily, and some bright-coloured ones can leach when wet.

Make sure your table mats and coasters all match, if you use them. You can select a design that is in keeping with the general theme of your B&B (for example, featuring local scenes or contemporary designs).

There are other things you will want to have on the table: will you provide salt and pepper shakers, for example, or salt and pepper mills? Think about your presentation of preserves: you may decide on using portioned packs of jams, small jars of jam, large jars, or homemade preserves and marmalades decanted into ramekin dishes, with spoons for serving. Butter may come in small pats, or may be served on a plate with a butter knife. Your style of presentation will need to match the general quality of your B&B. If you are aiming for a 5-star rating, then you need to consider an excellent standard of presentation for breakfast. If you are meeting a middle market of 3 stars, then a more standard approach may suffice. But, whatever style you adopt, you must make sure that it is consistent throughout.

Breakfast

The style and quality of breakfast that you offer will, to some extent, depend on the type of guests you attract. In this next section, we will look at types of breakfast and how subtle points can help create a more distinctive experience.

Nearly all visitors expect a B&B to provide a full cooked breakfast, but the dietary requirements of your guests will vary, and many will expect a vegetarian or continental-style breakfast. Whatever the type of breakfast, what and how much you provide will vary, although the quality, of course, should not. But the first question is, how will guests know what is available?

BREAKFAST MENUS

The idea of a breakfast menu may seem unnecessary. After all, you are there to talk to your guests and advise them verbally of the choices available; and your B&B is a home, after all, not a café. While that is all true, a menu can help guests to make choices while sitting and waiting for you to come out of the kitchen; and it can be a very useful way of emphasising the range and quality of what you offer. You can repeat the choices verbally, but it is good to have a printed version, too.

Where should you serve breakfast?
- HOW MANY TABLES?
- CROCKERY, CUTLERY, TABLEWARE

Breakfast
- BREAKFAST MENUS
- 'SELLING' BREAKFAST

You can present the menu on individual handwritten cards on the tables or mounted on the walls or blackboards. Alternatively, you could have printed and laminated cards in photograph frames, placed on the side buffet table. Always check menus for any stains, misspellings, or wear and tear: presentation is important, with menus as with any other element of your B&B.

A blank greeting card containing a handwritten menu, placed on the table, will instinctively be picked up by the guest. It will be more durable if laminated, and can add to the overall impression if it matches the style or theme of your B&B.

'SELLING' BREAKFAST
Look at these two examples of a breakfast menu:

Menu a

To Start

Cereal or juice

Full cooked

Toast

Tea or Coffee

Menu A lists the options available, but it may not inspire the guest. The choice of cereal or juice is quite limiting, and many guests may want both. Look at the words 'full cooked'. They do not describe the breakfast. As you travel around England, the definition of an English breakfast can vary. You may have a local speciality that will enhance the breakfast you offer: Lowestoft kippers, Lincolnshire or Cumberland sausage, Lancashire black pudding, to name a few. In almost all parts of the country you should be able to source local specialities, such as award-winning sausages, locally produced bacon, homemade preserves or local free-range eggs.

Breakfast

- BREAKFAST MENUS

- 'SELLING' BREAKFAST

Menu b

To Start

Please help yourself to freshly squeezed orange juice, yoghurt and cereals from the side table.

Main Course

Free range eggs
Fried, poached or scrambled

with local butcher's sausages, back bacon, home-grown tomatoes, mushrooms

or any combination

or

Boiled eggs with soldiers

or

Lowestoft kipper

or

Homemade smoked haddock fishcakes

Coffee

Freshly made ground or decaffeinated

Teas

Breakfast Blend, Assam, Darjeeling, China, Earl Grey, peppermint, camomile or fruit

Wholemeal and white toast served with homemade marmalade and jams.

Menu B, on the other hand, illustrates how menu descriptions can enhance the breakfast by highlighting the quality of the food you are offering. Let us look at the content of the menu in detail.

THE BUFFET SELECTION

The buffet selection is not specified in too much detail, so you will be free to vary the selection. You may not want to offer freshly squeezed juice, but may instead offer a choice of juices. Added choice can enhance quality. Should you, for example, have fruit juice pre-poured into small glasses or in jugs for self-service? The former may control the amount used, but the latter will allow guests to serve the amount they want. What range and styles of cereals will you provide? Small individual portion-sized boxes of cereal, large boxes, or other containers? Small boxes can again help you control portion, and can offer a wide selection, but you may find that the way in which they are supplied leaves you with lots of one type of cereal which no one likes it. Large boxes can offer variety, but can easily become crumpled. Using containers for cereals can look better, but it may leave guests uncertain of the brand quality. To correct this, some B&Bs place a label on the containers to promote the brand, and ensure that guests do not assume it is an economy brand. Whichever way you present cereals, consider the range available and think about offering some choices, including homemade muesli if you think that it would suit your operation.

COOKED BREAKFAST

Defining the options for cooked breakfast helps highlight the quality of the produce you use. Guests consider free-range eggs of higher quality than barn eggs, and often welcome a choice of styles of cooking. Sourcing locally made, butcher's-own sausages or locally reared bacon, can add distinctiveness to the menu, providing something the guests may never have tried before. If you can source award-winning items, then guests will have an even more favourable impression of the quality you are offering.

ALTERNATIVE OPTIONS

Providing slightly alternative options can also enhance the quality of the breakfast on offer. The next two options on Menu B – boiled eggs with soldiers and Lowestoft kipper – are both very traditional but slightly less-common breakfast items. Including them adds distinctiveness to your menu, and in the latter case emphasises a local speciality.

DISTINCTIVE OPTIONS

The final hot option on Menu B, homemade smoked haddock fishcakes, is a distinctive offering that is neither a local speciality nor a bought-in product, but a homemade item. Providing something homemade – whether it be smoked haddock fishcakes, jams, marmalades or bread – highlights extra attention to detail and additional care, and makes the menu memorable and enjoyable. Added to this, the smell of freshly baked bread, whether oven-baked or from a bread machine, creates an aroma that guests always appreciate.

Breakfast

– BREAKFAST MENUS

– 'SELLING' BREAKFAST

HOT DRINKS

You may have a wide range of hot drinks available at breakfast but, if they are all hidden in a kitchen cupboard, will the guest know what choices there are? Advertising the range of teas and types of coffee ensures that the guest knows the full range available and can make an informed choice.

TOAST

Toast is one of the fixtures of an English breakfast, but it must be of the right quality. Should you use a toast rack or a basket (this may depend on how much moisture the bread retains)? Could you offer a choice of breads? Could you offer homemade or speciality bakery items, such as croissants, pains au chocolat or bagels? Some B&Bs provide a toaster in the dining room so that guests may toast bread themselves. This can be more convenient, but can also limit the amount of service you offer, reduce the sense of customer care and have health and safety implications.

PRESERVES AND SPREADS

Marmalade and preserves in portioned plastic containers with peel-off lids can be perfect for convenience and portion control, but they are also difficult for some guests to use. Individual dishes or larger jars may be better, although you should remember to provide serving knives or spoons with larger jars. You may offer a choice of spreads, including butter and a low-fat spread, presented as portion packs, dishes or pats. If you plan to use portion packs always check the use-by date.

SAUCES AND EXTRAS

Sauces, too, can be served in individual portion packs or large bottles, but they need to look appealing, however you decide to serve them – almost empty sauce bottles, even if they have clean lids, will not add to the effect you are hoping to create. Do not limit guests to one type of milk either; offer them a choice between full-fat, semi-skimmed or skimmed milk (and there may be times when you need alternatives to these).

As with all these points, the choice of what you offer will very much depend on what works for you – and your guests. You may find it appropriate to add or remove the offer of alternatives, depending on the reactions of your general market.

Dining room ambience

A radio on in the background, possibly from your own kitchen, can provide news and traffic reports and help prevent stony silences and whispered conversations; it can at times help induce conversation between your guests. Not everyone will appreciate it, however, so it is worth monitoring guests' reaction.

Leaving a morning newspaper out, or the visitors' book, may be a good idea; many guests like to add their comments, and breakfast can be a convenient time for them to do this at leisure.

EVENING MEALS AND TAKEAWAYS

By this stage you will have decided whether to provide evening meals or not. If you do not intend to offer evening meals but are willing for guests to bring back take-away food, think about setting up a part of the dining room with cutlery, crockery and serviettes for this purpose. (After all, the last thing you will want is for them to be eating a curry in the bedroom, or any other food that has strong odours and the potential for leaving stains.) If the room is big enough, you could also supply a fridge and a microwave for the purpose of takeaways. Whatever you decide on, it is imperative you make your policy absolutely clear to your guests in advance.

CLEANLINESS

If you allow guests to eat takeaways in the dining room, you will need to make sure that it is clean and tidy before breakfast service, and that the air is free of any lingering odours. It is a good idea to clean the breakfast tables as soon after breakfast as possible. Leaving breakfast items out will look untidy and may leave guests with a poor impression of efficiency and hygiene. Reset the room as quickly as possible, ready for guests later that day. Dust every day, and polish and clean windows as necessary. Tidy books, magazines and vacuum the floor.

Lounge and extras

Guests will continue to use and appreciate a lounge, even when their bedrooms are equipped with TVs and chairs and you feel that they will no longer use a lounge. A lounge is a room for them to spend time in either before going out for the day or in the early evening; it also gives you somewhere to chat to guests in, and to serve tea on arrival – and very often it is this kind of personal contact that generates return visits. Where you have more than one bedroom and guests staying who know each other, to attend a wedding for example, a lounge is often a convenient meeting space in place of the bedrooms.

A lounge does not have to be large, but it must be comfortably furnished, with seating and lighting that are appropriate for varied use, such as reading and relaxing. As with bedrooms and bathrooms, there are extras that could be provided in the lounge to make the visitors' stay more comfortable. A desk with a controllable light and chair could be useful for the business traveller; a TV with video and DVDs, books and magazines, a CD player and board games are all possibilities.

Depending on the kind of B&B you run, the lounge may be used during the course of the day and at different times in the evening. In addition to your normal cleaning routine, the lounge may be worth checking regularly, if only to tidy books and magazines. If you are using a small table, coasters will prevent cup-marks.

Breakfast
- BREAKFAST MENUS
- 'SELLING' BREAKFAST

Dining room ambience
- EVENING MEALS AND TAKEAWAYS

Lounge and extras
- OTHER AREAS
- GUEST INFORMATION
- RECOMMENDING SOMEWHERE FOR DINNER
- A MEMENTO OF THE STAY
- ADDITIONAL POINTS
  – THE GARDEN

OTHER AREAS

All guests pass through the entrance hall with their luggage, so this is an area of the house that can take a lot of heavy wear. You will need to make sure that there is ample lighting, that it is easy for guests to navigate their way around any large pieces of furniture, and that decor and flooring are all in good order.

If you are planning to use this area for the registration of visitors, or for settling their bill, then you will need to provide a suitable desk or table.

GUEST INFORMATION

Whether guests are staying with you for work or pleasure, they may arrive in the area with little knowledge of what there is to see and do. The information you give them can make their stay more distinctive and enhance the overall quality of their experience.

Maps, comprehensive tourist information and guide books (possibly including walking maps) will all provide guests with ideas of places to visit and activities in the area. You could keep visitor attraction leaflets in an information rack, or in folders, or you could compile a series of suggested itineraries for days out, or walks from your front door. Itineraries could include driving tours of the area, with routes and suggestions of places to stop. You could highlight lesser-known places of interest and suggest convenient stops for lunch or a cream tea. For more information go to visitbritain.com

---

Case Study
A local touring itinerary for the guests

This is an example of a local touring itinerary produced by a rural B&B, which guests holidaying in the area could use if they choose. Some B&Bs prepare a number of these, personalise them ('Mr & Mrs Smith, some ideas for a sunny day!') and print them off from their PC. Each itinerary can have a theme such as Interesting Gardens, Historic Houses and a Good Pub Lunch, A Steam Railway and a Riverside Walk, A Bird Reserve with Binoculars, Boating with a Cream Tea.

Case Study

A day out from the Grange

Take the A134 and drive 2 miles to Lavenham. The market place is in the centre of this medieval wool village where you will also find parking. From the Tourist Information Centre in Lady Street (just off the market place) you can hire an audio walking guide – and at your own pace see the magnificent timber-framed buildings, Corpus Christi guildhall (NT) and the glorious, high-towered 16th-century church. There are plenty of galleries, interesting shops and a wide range of pubs, teashops and restaurants to visit on the route.

Leave Lavenham on the A1141 towards Sudbury and, passing the church on the right, take the minor road signposted to Long Melford. The village is famous as the location for the filming of the Lovejoy TV series.

The main street (1 mile) is the longest village street in England and has numerous antique shops. There are two historic houses here – Long Melford Hall (NT) and Kentwell Hall, a moated Elizabethan mansion, which is renowned for its annual Tudor Recreations. Hidden away at the top of the village green is the beautiful Holy Trinity church.

Travel south on the A311 to Sudbury, birthplace of Thomas Gainsborough. A bronze statue of the artist is prominent in the market place, where you can also park and follow the signposts to Gainsborough's House. Now a museum and gallery, it displays an amazing collection of his work. After a tour of the house you can relax in the walled garden and café.

Take the B1071 out of Sudbury and through the village of Boxford until you branch off towards Kersey, a picturesque village famous for the water splash across the street. Look out for the ducks as you drive through it! At the top of the hill is yet another high-towered church, St Mary's. Leave on the minor road signposted towards Lavenham, only 6 miles away. If you feel the need for a cream tea, call in en route at Corncraft in Monks Eleigh.

Lounge and extras

- OTHER AREAS

- GUEST INFORMATION

- RECOMMENDING SOMEWHERE FOR DINNER

- A MEMENTO OF THE STAY

- ADDITIONAL POINTS – THE GARDEN

Make use of your knowledge of local footpaths and bridleways for your walking maps, creating short and long walks, a 'red' and a 'blue' trail, a 20-minute stroll or an hour-long walk. Depending on your location, you could even suggest a two-mile jogging route.

An Ordnance Survey (OS) map of your area is a very useful way of showing places of interest. The OS can produce a bespoke map with your property at its centre (be careful if you are located by the coast, otherwise half of the map will feature the sea!). This can be framed and hung on the wall as a reference for guests. Around the map you could place the leaflets of local attractions, and indicate where each is, either with a number or by connecting the leaflet to its location with a length of thread.

RECOMMENDING SOMEWHERE FOR DINNER

One question you will usually be asked by guests is 'Can you recommend somewhere for dinner?' This is a difficult question to answer, for what you like may not match the guests' tastes. Some guests want an inexpensive meal in a friendly pub, while others may want a fine dining experience in a local restaurant. See case study on p. 95.

One thing you could do is create a folder of local menus. These could be collected on a reciprocal arrangement: you promote the establishment by promoting their menu, and in return the establishment could promote your B&B by displaying your card. The folder could contain a variety of menus from local pubs, restaurants and cafés to suit a wide range of tastes and needs. If you don't mind people bringing a takeaway back, include some takeaway menus as well.

A local map, displayed on the wall, could give the location of local eateries. These could be highlighted with a number, or by linking their business card to their location, again with a length of thread. If the menu folder is in a public area such as a lounge or entrance hallway, you could add a blank page alongside each menu, headed 'Guests' Feedback', and leave your guests to make comments on each place.

A MEMENTO OF THE STAY

Many guests like to take away a reminder of their stay. If you make homemade jams or other items, you could display these for sale, or you could give a postcard of your B&B as a reminder. Handing out a business card to guests as they leave will remind them both to come back and also to recommend you to others.

ADDITIONAL POINTS — THE GARDEN

If visitors are able to use the garden, providing garden chairs, benches, tables, sun umbrellas, lighting and sand buckets for smokers can all help make them feel that they are welcome to sit and relax. If there are any restrictions on where guests can go, make sure that these are clear.

These areas will also need regular care and maintenance. It will not always be possible to make sure that the toys and play equipment of a young family are hidden from view, but try to keep them away from the guests' access route to the main entrance.

Sweep paths and check them for uneven surfaces. A garden may not be a feature you make available to your guests, but you will need to keep it tidy and free of weeds. If the garden is available to your guests, you will need to make sure that any garden furniture, especially seating, is clean and safe.

Departure

Your visitors have stayed, eaten breakfast and are now ready to depart. What do you do? Are you there to see them leave? Do you need to present them with a bill? How will they expect to pay? Will they expect a receipt?

Knowing the guest's intended date of departure gives you an opportunity to prepare their bill in advance. You could leave it folded, with their name on, at their place-setting for breakfast, have it prepared in an envelope on the hall table, or present it to them as they are about to depart.

A numbered invoice book will be perfectly acceptable for the bill, and will be helpful for your accounts. Alternatively, headed paper has the added advantage of acting as a helpful reminder of their stay with you. Bear in mind that business guests will expect a receipt for expenses claims.

Many guests will be happy to pay with either cash or a personal cheque. Some B&Bs with a lot of business guests now take credit cards, but they are still the exception. Accepting credit cards will cost you, so you will need to weigh up the pros and cons carefully before deciding.

This might be your last opportunity to engage with your visitors and encourage them to return. As on their arrival, offer them assistance with their luggage, if they have not already brought it down to pay their bill.

You will also want to generate repeat and recommendation business, so you may want to think about giving departing guests a reminder of your B&B in the form of a pot of homemade preserve, clearly labelled with your B&B's name and telephone number, or perhaps even a pen or key ring.

If you feel this is not appropriate, make sure that each guest leaves with a copy of your brochure or a small business card. After all, each guest who has a good stay is a potential ambassador for your business. A business card will act as a useful prompt to them.

Finally, just before they leave, check that they have given you back the room keys.

Next steps

The next chapter looks at ways in which you can start to grow your business, including what you should be doing to track your business through your first full season of trading, and how you could use this information to help formulate ideas for continued growth. Even if you have found the first year very busy, it is still important to know how business came to you, what advertising worked, and whether there may be any other ideas to stimulate business. Being busy today is not always a guarantee of being busy tomorrow.

Chapter 8
Growing the business

Let's hope that, after your first year in business, you will be able to say that you are enjoying the experience. You will probably have met some very interesting people, enjoyed working from home, and found it a varied and interesting lifestyle.

You may now want to look at ways in which you can develop the business further. But before you start looking forward, it is first worth looking back. Knowing how your guests found your B&B, what made them stay and whether they enjoyed their stay are three important ways of monitoring your business.

Review the year

HOW DID YOUR GUESTS FIND YOUR B&B?

How guests came to choose your B&B is an important question that you need to try to ask each guest at the outset. You could ask the question on arrival, but you will need to keep a record to track how business came to you.

In Chapter 5 we saw how you could use a registration form to find the answer to this question. The registration form can become a very useful marketing tool for you. It allows you to gather information from your guest without being overly officious or standing over them as they complete the form. By leaving the form in the bedroom, with a pen lying across it, and simply requesting that they complete it in their own time, you can keep a precise record of which forms of advertising are working and which are not.

Review the year
- HOW DID YOUR GUESTS FIND YOUR B&B?
- GETTING FEEDBACK
- KEEPING IN TOUCH

The forms may also be used to keep a record of your guests – for example, whether they had any dietary requirements, preferred the room overlooking the garden, needed extra desk space, or merely what brought them to your area. Forms can act as a reminder to you to put a returning guest in their favourite room, or get some of their favourite tea for breakfast. These little touches can have a big impact on a guest.

GETTING FEEDBACK

One good way of getting feedback is to use a guest comment book. Many guests are happy to record a few thoughts at the end of their stay. You will almost certainly receive many pleasant comments and it is always pleasant to read how much guests enjoyed staying with you. Nevertheless, it can also be useful to know more specifically how the guests found their stay. Was the bed comfortable? Did the lighting work? Was the room too noisy? You could use a guest feedback book or card to find out whether everything worked well, whether the room was easy to use, and whether anything might have made the guests feel better about their stay. This, like the registration form, can be left in the bedroom for guests to complete in their own time. Not every guest will complete it, but from the ones who do you will quickly build up a clear picture of how they see your B&B.

Another good question to ask certain guests is what they liked most about the B&B. It is a good question to add on the feedback form, as it will ask guests to focus on what the most special feature or most memorable part of the B&B was. It is often surprising what guests say. It may not be the fact that you have a swimming pool in the garden, or have put widescreen TVs in each bedroom. Instead, it may be the view from the bedroom window, the quality of your breakfast or the fact that there is plenty of off-road parking. We will look at why this information is so important shortly; for the time being, the important message is that what you may feel is special about your B&B may not match your guests' impressions.

KEEPING IN TOUCH

As everyone knows, the best form of business is repeat business, but how do you keep guests returning? You could consider sending a Christmas card or even a New Year card to guests who you have a good rapport with and to the ones you would like to see return. A New Year card can be useful, as it is more likely to be kept after the Christmas cards have been discarded. But you need also to bear in mind that sending cards will not be suitable or necessary for all guests.

Review the year

- HOW DID YOUR GUESTS FIND YOUR B&B?

- GETTING FEEDBACK

- KEEPING IN TOUCH

Developing the business

Developing the business

- STEP 1 – DEVELOPING YOURSELF

- STEP 2 – DEVELOPING YOUR PROPERTY

STEP 1 – DEVELOPING YOURSELF

Even within a small business such as a B&B, learning new skills can contribute significantly to the development of your business. Contact your local TIC or tourist organisation for advice on suitable courses in your area. They may be able to put you in touch with your local Tourism Officer, regional tourist board, or the tourism section of your regional development agency. Many of these organisations co-ordinate, or know of, a variety of courses throughout the year that are designed specifically for smaller tourism businesses. Courses can cover disability awareness, brochure design, bookkeeping skills, and also include the Welcome to Excellence family of courses. The Welcome courses are an excellent way to develop your understanding of customer care.

STEP 2 – DEVELOPING YOUR PROPERTY

After your first year, and after the first quality assessment, you should ask yourself whether you should try to improve the overall quality of the B&B and the grade achieved. Use the assessor's visit and guidance to consider whether you could develop quality standards, but don't go chasing ratings or accolades for the sake of them. Quality development should be done to match guests' needs, and raise your profile accordingly. Planned quality development can sometimes lead to business development.

ENHANCE YOUR RATING

If at the time of your assessment you were told that you were close to a higher quality grade, then ask yourself whether reaching that grade will be good for your business. Sometimes it may not be. Take as an example a 4-star B&B that is close to achieving 5 stars. This is the highest rating a B&B can have, but guests at that level may have very high expectations. If you match or exceed those expectations, then the guest should be happy; if you miss them, they may be disappointed. Sometimes, promising less but delivering more can work better, and being at the top end of 1 star band, rather than at the lower end of another, can be good for your business.

ACHIEVE AN ACCOLADE

Instead of chasing a higher grade, it may be more appropriate to obtain an accolade. In the star scheme there are two accolades awarded to B&Bs. A Silver accolade is given to accommodation that offers an excellent experience in guest comfort and customer care. A Gold accolade is awarded to those B&Bs where the experience is exceptional. Your assessor will be able to advise more exactly on Silver and Gold awards at the time of your assessment.

Two accreditations that show that your property meets the needs of walkers and cyclist are Walkers Welcome and Cyclist Welcome. Again, your assessor will be able to offer advice on these at the time of your assessment.

IDENTIFY GUESTS' NEEDS

The feedback form is useful for finding out what your guests need. You may have started your B&B expecting lots of guests on holiday or on weekend breaks, and furnished and styled your rooms accordingly. Now, after a full season or year in business, you realise that many of your guest are actually working in the area, possibly on business or as contractors.

You can use the feedback forms to decide whether you need to restyle your rooms, add anything, or even remove items. Consider, for example, the needs of a business traveller staying in a bedroom designed for leisure guests. There may be a dressing table with a stool, a table mirror, lamp and various items to dress the table; a clothes brush, tissues, ornaments and a vase of flowers. The table may look very attractive, but will it be functional for the business traveller? You could keep the general appearance of the table but slightly de-clutter it, then replace the stool with a chair and ensure that there are power points close by. If there are no fixed points, you could add an extension lead to provide points. By doing this, you will now allow the business traveller to use the dressing table as a desk, plug in their laptop, recharge their mobile phone, and work in comfort.

Similarly, you may now realise that a range of OS maps, a spare pair of binoculars and the offer of tumble-drying wet clothes are useful extras to offer to guests who are walking or bird-watching.

Developing a more accessible B&B

In Chapter 3 we looked at various laws that could affect the way in which you run your B&B. One such law is the Disability Discrimination Act (DDA). Accessibility is not a new concern: numerous operators have complied with the spirit of the DDA for many years, by adapting their properties to cater for disabled guests. Many will have done this to meet the needs of the market. Meeting the needs of the DDA is a legal requirement, but it can also be good for your business.

If you doubt this, look at the following facts:

- There are 9 million disabled people in this country – one in six of us.
- 2.7 million disabled people travel regularly in this country, and they travel with friends, family and carers. The entire market contains over 15 million people – a quarter of the population.
- It is estimated that the market has a spending power of over £50 billion.
- 5% of disabled people use wheelchairs.
- Only 12% of us have 20:20 vision.
- Half of all disabled people in the UK are over 65.
- By 2011, 30% of the population will be over 55.
- The over-50s possess 80% of the UK's wealth.

The principal symbol used to denote the disabled market is the wheelchair, but disabilities are varied and include learning difficulties and disabilities, visual impairment, hearing impairment, arthritis, asthma, diabetes and a range of physical conditions. Millions of people have a temporary disability, for example, a broken limb, and pregnant women have access needs. The disabled market is a strong market, and research shows that disabled travellers are loyal customers.

NATIONAL ACCESSIBLE SCHEME

VisitBritain's National Accessible Scheme (NAS) recognises and identifies B&Bs that meet the needs of disabled guests.

The NAS assesses the suitability of accommodation against three types of disability: mobility, visual and hearing. The scheme contains criteria to help each type of disability, and you can achieve a rating to help promote your business more readily to the disabled market. There are four standards that can be achieved for mobility, two standards for visual, and two standards for hearing. It may be that you cannot achieve a rating against all the standards, nor attain the most involved rating within each standard, but you might be able to meet some of the criteria for some of the schemes. There will always be some adaptations you can make. To aid you further, there is a self-assessment pack that accompanies the standards. This allows you to assess your own property against the three standards, and helps you formulate an action plan for future developments.

For further information about the NAS, please contact Quality in Tourism on 0845 3006996, or email qualityintourism@gslglobal.com

Step 3 – Repeats and referrals

Repeat business is often the best type of business, but recommended and referral business come a close second. If your guest has had a good stay, you would hope that they would recommend you to friends, family and colleagues. To make this more likely to happen, make sure that no guest leaves you without a copy of your brochure or business card. Include it with the bill at the end of their stay.

Referral business can come from other B&Bs and accommodation in your area. We mentioned in Chapter 2 the idea of contacting other B&Bs in your area, as you get ready to launch your business. You should consider joining a more formal association exists, if one exists. The opportunity to meet other like-minded people who are having similar experiences to you will prove invaluable. You will be able to swap notes, compare bookings and pick up new ideas. Local associations can help you discover whether you are not as busy as everyone else, and are possibly missing an opportunity. You may be able to visit other B&Bs in the association and understand where you fit in to the local picture.

Being able to visit local B&Bs can be very useful, should you receive an enquiry for a night when you are already full. If you know your colleagues, you can refer calls with confidence, knowing they will get a similar experience to staying with you. And this works equally the other way round. If other B&Bs know your property, the style of your accommodation and the number and size of your rooms, they too can refer business to you with confidence and reassurance.

Local associations can also provide a very useful way of bulk-purchasing various items, such as toiletries and other guest accessories, thereby reducing your outgoings.

Step 4 – Raising your local profile

Raising your local profile may seem a strange idea. After all, you are trying to encourage guests to visit from a long distance away, not from your own doorstep. And yet the local market can prove very fruitful.

Guests visiting friends and relations often depend on these friends and relatives making the booking. It is good practice to be known locally to capture this business, for example by advertising in a local parish or village magazine, or the local newspaper.

If you have a business card, a postcard of your property or a brochure, you could distribute these locally where they

Developing a more accessible B&B

– NATIONAL ACCESSIBLE SCHEME

Step 3 – Repeats and referrals

Step 4 – Raising your local profile

will be seen. You may be able to place them in the local post office, shops, pubs, garages or the newsagent. Often this can be a reciprocal arrangement: if pubs have your card in their bar, you can reciprocate by promoting their menu in your bedroom folder.

Take advantage of the events that bring people to your area. Organisations for which weddings are important business – for example, a company that plans weddings, a wedding-cake maker, or caterers – may all receive requests from the wedding party for advice on places to stay, and may welcome your details. Similarly, you might visit your local estate agent and see whether they would be willing to pass on your details to people who are moving home and who may want to stay in an area to see whether it suits them.

You will find the local TIC a very useful point of contact: they can be extremely effective in promoting your B&B. They may or may not generate bookings, but the exposure they provide can be invaluable, and you should build a close relationship with them even if they have sent you only a number of guests over the year. If you wanted to help them match suitable properties to the enquiries they receive, you could invite the staff round for a coffee morning and show them round, or take in some photographs of your property so they can see what it looks like. Keep them advised on availability and go to any open days or leaflet swaps they organise.

The travelling business market can also provide you with accommodation bookings throughout the year. It can be useful to identify any local companies that need accommodation for staff attending their offices for meetings or training courses. There are tremendous opportunities for attracting the business market. Contact various companies to ask whether they ever require accommodation for staff. There is no point sending your details to the managing director if it is the head of HR who makes the bookings; find out who is responsible for making bookings, and then send them your details.

Step 5 – Developing your marketing

If this is your first year running a B&B, your marketing and promotion may have been limited to creating a simple brochure or business card and then, in the course of the year, placing an advertisement in a local magazine. Now that your business is beginning to move forward, it could be worth thinking about new marketing ideas.

Step 5 – Developing
your marketing
- DEVELOPING YOUR
  BROCHURE
- DEVELOP A WEBSITE
- ADVERTISING
- PLAN THE YEAR

DEVELOPING YOUR BROCHURE
Chapter 4 looked in detail at design ideas for a brochure, but it is now worth looking at the brochure again and considering how well it works. Does it need to be changed? You could have your brochure professionally printed, and use photographs taken by a commercial photographer; or you could develop a brochure yourself by using a digital camera and an office stationery company. Whatever you decide, for your brochure to sell your B&B, it will have to have impact.

Think about the feedback your guests gave you about what they thought was the most special or memorable aspect of your property. It may have been the bedroom, the bathroom or the garden. If a picture really is worth a thousand words, include photographs of those features. You may need to show a number of features, including the frontage of the house, the bedrooms and the bathrooms. But based on the feedback you received, you may want to include a photograph of a plate of cooked breakfast, the view out of the bedroom window – even yourself! Try to use one main image within the brochure, and select the image that best sums up your B&B.

If you have developed a website, add the address to the new brochure, and don't forget to promote your quality rating.

DEVELOP A WEBSITE
You receive free entry onto www.visitbritain.com and www.enjoyengland.com, the official tourism websites for Britain and England, once you have been assessed by VisitBritain. If you now decide to have your own website, you can have a link from the VisitBritain websites to your own.

If you do not have a website, now may be the time to think about developing one. It need not be expensive, and you may even consider building it yourself. With your own website you can update information immediately, refresh photographs as the seasons or property change, and show your B&B in much more detail than is possible in a brochure.

An alternative to developing a website of your own (if you think this is going to prove too expensive) is to be included on a local B&B association site – it would be worth finding out how much this costs.

ADVERTISING

One of the benefits of being assessed by VisitBritain is a free listing in the Enjoy England official guides to quality, which have international distribution. This may provide you with all the exposure you need, or you may decide you need to advertise elsewhere as well. Advertising in local accommodation or regional guides may be useful. You can visit your TIC for more advice on local guides.

Advertising elsewhere can be expensive, especially for smaller businesses, but you may need to do it. Keep your advertising truthful (bear in mind the Trade Descriptions Act), but use information that generates interest and appeal to create awareness of your B&B. Use your rating: it can attract attention quickly and highlights the fact that you have an official endorsement.

If a significant proportion of your visitors come from a certain geographical area, obtain a local newspaper and consider advertising in it. The newspaper may regularly carry features on your region, and may even have a special advertising rate.

Two points to bear in mind are that a single advertisement is unlikely to have a great impact, and that the effect of advertising can be cumulative – so an advertisement may need to be repeated. Take account of this in your advertising budget, but then stick to the budget.

PLAN THE YEAR

A marketing and advertising calendar can help you plan your year and spread your costs. Mark months with relevant activity to be sure you don't miss deadlines. Regional and local accommodation guides tend to go to printers in the autumn to be ready for distribution before the end of the year, so information is usually collected in the summer. If you want to be included, you'll have to get your entry in by then. This will usually include a fee. If you have a set budget for the year and want to spread costs out, highlight this as being a high-cost period.

Find out about annual events, festivals and activities, such as county shows, motor racing and trade fairs, and mark these on your calendar. An enquiry made ten months in advance for just one night on what appears to be a quiet weekend in February may be to attend an event that lasts three days and will attract thousands of visitors to your area. You may want to hold out for a three-night booking. You may also want to contact the organisers of the event and find out how they promote and advertise the event. You could possibly advertise in their programme, which could be another way of publicising your B&B.

Next steps

In the next chapter we look at problems and solutions. Most owners find that their B&Bs run smoothly, but every now and again you may confront a situation for which there is no immediate or obvious solution. The next chapter looks at a variety of situations and offers guidance on how to handle them.

Step 5 – Developing
your marketing

- DEVELOPING YOUR
  BROCHURE

- DEVELOP A WEBSITE

- ADVERTISING

- PLAN THE YEAR

Chapter 9

Some common problems

This short chapter highlights some issues that occasionally arise with B&B operators, looking at prevention as well as at cure. It is true to say that with most well-run B&Bs, problems are the exception rather than the rule.

How to deal with problems

Things occasionally go wrong in B&Bs, and people make complaints, as they do in any business. What may be harder for you is that you are running your B&B from your own home, and it will be difficult not to take complaints personally. You must nevertheless try to be objective. Be courteous at all times and listen to what it being said – no matter how unjustified you feel the complaint is, try not to make a counter-argument before you have heard the other person's side. After all, there are always two sides to every complaint.

By listening and not interrupting you will at least make guests realise that you are taking the issue seriously. Your body language will also be important: gestures may either inflame the situation or help to diffuse it. If it is possible, ask the guest to go somewhere private, so that other guests or family members do not hear the discussion. And complaints can be useful: a polite complaint gives you the opportunity to put things right or to take remedial actions and turn a situation around.

No shows

Occasionally a guest does not arrive – this is commonly known as a 'no show' – or a pre-booked guest cancels their reservation on the day, or checks out early. All of these could potentially break the contract that you had made with the customer.

What precautions can you take? When a guest makes a reservation, make sure that you have advised them of your cancellation policy (this is discussed in Chapter 5 under 'Deposits' and 'Response to bookings'). A cancellation policy forms part of the contract that you make with the visitor, and it is always a good idea to send a copy to them (if there is time before their visit). If for any reason you have omitted to tell them about your policy, you may still be entitled to make a charge.

No shows

There are various reasons that guests will give for cancelling bookings and you need to judge how to handle each. You may consider it inappropriate to follow through a charge when a close relative has died, or when there has been a serious road accident en route. But there are other frustrating examples of a 'late change in plans' that leave you carrying the potential loss. One such example is when guests at a local wedding are offered accommodation with friends or family and phone you in the early evening to say they do not need the room any longer. This is pretty contemptible behaviour, and you may reasonably have the same opinion of these bookings as you do of those that fail to arrive, without giving a reason.

Where you feel that you should charge, it is best to stick to your policy and not levy what has been called an irritation charge, even though you may feel it would be appropriate. People have varying success in recovering costs, but the best advice is to be factual, business-like and timely. Any bill that you send should have a covering letter that states when the booking was made (it is always a good idea to record this in your booking diary) and by whom. As you are unlikely to have been able to re-let the accommodation in the case of a no-show or very late cancellation, you could add a line to the covering letter that states that you were 'unable to re-let the room and had previously refused other bookings because I was holding your booking' (if this is the case).

If a guest cancels a booking or checks out early, they are in breach of the booking contract they have with you.

This is the procedure to follow if you want to make a claim for damages:

What should I do first? You must first make every reasonable effort to minimise your loss by trying to re-let the accommodation. (If you re-let the room at the same price, you should have no loss and so cannot make a claim.)

What amount can I claim? If, despite your efforts, you cannot re-let the accommodation, you will be entitled to claim damages that reflect the losses you have actually incurred as a result of the cancellation. This is the value of the booking, or the part of it for which the accommodation could not be re-let, less the value of any items included in the price which you did not have the expense of supplying, such as food, light, heat and service charge. You should note that there is a general rule of thumb that the loss will amount to about two-thirds of the value of the booking, but individual cases differ and there can be no hard-and-fast rules.

What about the deposit? You may keep the deposit, setting it off against the amount claimed.

How soon can you make a claim? You must wait until the period of the booking has elapsed before you can send the guest an invoice for the amount claimed, for example in the case of two rooms for a three-day weekend.

Receiving payment can sometimes require a little persistence, and you may need to send a reminder by recorded delivery. Bear in mind that you can recover costs with damages as a small claim through the courts: a small claim can be for any amount up to £5,000. Some operators have successfully done this, but you may also want to consider the amounts involved before taking that step – you will have to pay a fee to start your claim, although this will be added to the money that you are already owed if your claim is successful. Despite the costs involved, it can sometimes be useful to remind people who rightfully owe you payment that you have the option to take this line of action.

No shows

The appropriate forms and a booklet advising you on how to pursue your claim can be obtained from any county court.

Over-bookings

Over-bookings

- MORE GUESTS THAN
BOOKED

Just as awkwardly, there are times when a double booking has been made and you have no rooms available. A frequent cause of this happening is when other family members take bookings and forget to tell you, so the first thing to stress is that everyone needs to understand how important it is to record all details. What do you do in this situation? As with a 'no show', double booking is a breach of contract and the guest is legally entitled to make a claim. You would hope to be able to resolve it, but it may not always be possible to do so.

What you should do in this situation is to try to find them suitable alternative accommodation nearby – you will no doubt have a contact list of other B&B operators, and it is always best to try to find somewhere that is similar to your style of B&B, if possible. If you are, for example, in a rural farm location, offering the visitors a busy pub on a main road may not be a welcome alternative. Legally the guest can claim for any extra costs incurred, so you will be liable for any difference in tariff charges. However, if the guest declines any of your suggestions, they cannot book themselves into a five-star hotel and expect you to pay the difference!

MORE GUESTS THAN BOOKED

A different kind of problem with over-booking is when more guests arrive than were booked – for example, you have a booking for a twin room and then three visitors arrive. All your other rooms are occupied.

First check your reservations file for details of the booking, and a copy of any written confirmation. If your file does not include any support details, one of you will have made a genuine mistake – so how should you proceed?

Do not blame the guests. Rather, see if there is a solution that they will be able to accept. If they are prepared to be split up, for example, you could, again, contact other B&B providers nearby (either on your own, or on the guest's behalf) to find a single room. If, however, they insist on being together, you may need to find alternative accommodation for everyone.

There is no point in worrying too much about something that may never happen. If you have a problem with over-booking, it will be a situation where all parties are present, and ingenuity and compromise may well present the solution. It's not possible to look at all permutations; for the moment, all you need to be aware of is that this is an area where things can go awry.

Non-acceptance of the accommodation

What happens when a guest refuses to accept the accommodation that they have booked? The answer to this question depends on the reason for the refusal. If the room does not, for example, have the four-poster bed or the Jacuzzi bath that had been booked, the guest could possibly be able to claim against you under the Trade Descriptions Act (referred to in Chapter 3). If however, they refuse the accommodation because they consider it too small, try to see if there is an alternative way to resolve the issue. In this case, if you cannot arrive at an acceptable solution, you may be entitled to treat this as a cancellation.

Late arrivals

When you accept a booking, it is always a good idea to note the approximate time that guests will arrive, so taking telephone contact numbers is important – particularly a mobile number. As you are running a B&B and not a hotel, it is also quite appropriate for you to ask guests to phone if they are unduly delayed. Some people will automatically ring to let you know that they are running late or that they are held up in traffic.

What should you do if a guest who is booked in for six o'clock has not made contact or left a message for you by eleven o'clock?

Go to bed! It is unlikely that the guest will arrive in the early hours and try to wake you by banging on the front door. It is possible, though, that either the guest or you may have got the wrong date. Contact them as soon as possible the next day. Depending on the circumstances, you may need to consider what charge you will make.

Over-bookings

– MORE GUESTS THAN BOOKED

Non-acceptance of the accommodation

Late arrivals

Early arrivals

Early arrivals

Sometimes visitors book your accommodation because they are attending a wedding in the area. Wedding guests often expect to be able to arrive early to change before the ceremony (depending on the time of the wedding, of course), and may want to use an iron or prepare themselves in some other way. The information that you send, or verbally confirm, when the booking is made must spell out the times that they can arrive – unless you want to make accommodating arrangements, where you think it appropriate. Bear in mind, too, that many weddings and celebration parties are held on Saturdays, that the guests may often return late and that they will perhaps not be up in time for breakfast on Sundays. You may need to bend your own 'rules' to find a compromise that suits all.

What do you do if visitors break your policies?

What do you do if visitors break your policies?

You may have a policy not to take pets or allow smoking in your home. This will form part of your advertising and your booking procedures, so that prospective guests should be clear about where you stand on these issues. So what do you do when it becomes evident to you that a guest is smoking cigarettes in their bedroom?

You are entirely within your rights to question the guest about this, remind them of the policy and ask them not to smoke. Whether you ask them to leave is a matter for your discretion, although you can do so only if the guest had clearly understood your policy on arrival. (If you want to be doubly sure about this, put a sign up in the bedroom.) A statement of your policies need not be in the form of a draconian 'Rules of this House'. It could be in the shape of two small 'tent cards' that need not look out of place, and should reassure your non-smoking guests. Sometimes the subtle absence of an ashtray is not enough.

Damage to, or loss of, your property and possessions

Accidents will happen in your B & B. You will have to treat it as part of the expected wear and tear of a B & B that from time to time guests will break an ornament or knock over a bedside light. Guests will more often than not let you know they have done something like this straightaway. But sometimes they will be embarrassed, and you will not notice the damage until you service the room (this is just one of the reasons for checking that everything is working when you clean the room). You will probably decide to take most of these breakages in your stride, but there will be some that you feel you cannot ignore. Some of these, such as a flood caused by a running tap and water damage to flooring, will be covered by your insurance policy. But what about when you discover the iron mark on the carpet or bedlinen, especially if you do so after the guest has paid and departed? In such circumstances, contact the guest immediately and follow your contact up with an invoice and a quotation for the cost of repairing or replacing the item.

You could take the same approach when something is missing. It is very rare that guests steal items from B&Bs, but occasionally they take things inadvertently – towels, for example. If this happens, contact the guest (who is likely to be very embarrassed) and see whether they can find and return the missing item. Only if they cannot, or if they show no inclination to try to do so, should you send an invoice and quotation.

If you are sure something has been stolen, rather than taken by accident, you should contact the police immediately.

Dietary requirements

Most visitors will tell you they have special dietary requirements in advance, but sometimes a guest comes into the dining room and tells you that there is little on your menu, or that you offer, that they can eat – because they are on, for example, a gluten-free diet. They may be convinced that they told you when they booked; you are equally sure that they did not. This is a time when it might be politic to accept that 'the customer is (nearly) always right'.

In this kind of circumstance, it helps to be resourceful or have a suitable alternative that can be easily or quickly prepared – fruit compote or fresh fruit in place of cereal, some long-life, skimmed or non-dairy milk. The list of alternatives need not be a long one, but it will be a reassurance to you, and a demonstration to your guests that you are attempting to anticipate their needs.

* * *

These are some of the problems that can occur in B&Bs, but they are far from being everyday ones. The day-to-day running of England's B&Bs follows a successful formula that is based on genuine hospitality enjoyed by thousands of delighted guests each year. If you are one of the happy band of operators, you will know what the rewards can be, especially when you can tap into a good market.

If you have read this far, you are likely to be about to embark on your new venture. Good luck with it. We are confident that you will have a wonderful experience, and we hope that this guide has given you an insight into the kind of life ahead of you!

Damage to, or loss of, your property and possessions

Dietary requirements

Sources of further help

There are various organisations responsible for managing tourism in England: VisitBritain covers all of England, while the regional tourism delivery partners cover their respective regions. From your point of view, however, your first point of contact should always be your local or nearest Tourist Information Centre (TIC). TICs (sometimes called 'visitor information centres') operate at a local level and should be able to put you in touch with a local, district or county tourism officer.

Your tourism officer may be able to give you the best advice on local tourism matters, including any tourism initiatives, local associations and groups, as well as local or regional guides and publications.

Here is a list of some of the main tourism-related organisations in England.

National Tourist Board

VisitBritain

Thames Tower
Black's Road
London
W6 9EL

Tel: 020 8846 9000
Fax: 020 8563 0302
www.visitbritain.com
www.enjoyengland.com

National Quality Assurance Schemes (NQAS)

For information on how to join VisitBritain's NQAS contact:
Quality in Tourism
Farncombe House
Farncombe
Broadway
WR12 7LJ
Tel: 0845 300 6996
Fax: 01386 854319
www.qualityintourism.co.uk

Regional Tourist Boards

Northumbria

One NorthEast Tourism Team
Stella House
Goldcrest Way
Newburn Riverside
Newcastle upon Tyne
NE15 8NY
www.tourismnortheast.co.uk

North West

Cumbria Tourist Board
Ashleigh
Holly Road
Windermere
LA23 2AQ
Tel: 015394 4444
Fax: 015394 44041
www.cumbriatourism.info

Lancashire & Blackpool Tourist Board
St George's House
St George's Street
Chorley
PR7 2AA
www.visitlancashire.com

Marketing Manchester
Churchgate House
56 Oxford Street
Manchester
M1 6EU
www.visitmanchester.com

The Mersey Partnership
12 Princes Dock
Princes Parade
Liverpool
L3 1BG
www.visitliverpool.com

Cheshire & Warrington Tourism Board
Grosvenor Park Lodge
Grosvenor Park Road
Chester
CH1 1QQ
www.visit-cheshire.com

Yorkshire

Yorkshire Tourist Board
312 Tadcaster Rd
York
YO24 1GS
Tel: 01904 702 000
Fax: 01904 701 414
www.yorkshiretouristboard.net

East Midlands

East Midlands Tourism
Apex Court
City Link
Nottingham
NG2 4LA
www.emda.org.uk/tourism/tourism

West Midlands

Heart of England Tourism
Woodside
Larkhill Road
Worcester
WR5 2EZ
www.visitheartofengland.com

East of England

East of England Tourist Board
Toppesfield Hall
Hadleigh
Suffolk
IP7 5DN
Tel: 01473 822922
Fax: 01473 823063
www.eetb.org.uk

London

London Tourist Board & Convention Board
1 Warwick Row
London
SW1E 5ER
Tel: 020 7932 2000
Fax: 020 7932 0222
www.visitlondon.com

South East

Tourism South East
40 Chamberlayne Road
Eastleigh
Hampshire
SO50 5JH
www.visitsoutheastengland.com

South West

South West Tourism
Woodwater Park
Pynes Hill
Exeter
EX2 5WT
Tel: 0870 442 0830
Fax: 0870 442 0840
www.swtourism.co.uk

The Pink Booklet

For advice on all legal aspects connected with setting up and running a B&B, you may want to consult the *Pink Booklet*. The *Pink Booklet* is available from VisitBritain on 0870 606 7204.

Disability Discrimination Act (DDA)

For more information on the Disability Discrimination Act and help with good business practice, contact the Disability Rights Commission's (DRC) helpline on 08457 622 633 (text phone 08457 622 644). The DRC's websites are www.drc-gb.org and www.open4all.org
DRC Helpline
FREEPOST
MID 02164
Stratford upon Avon
CV37 9BR

Tourism for All UK is the national charity offering a central
source of travel and holiday information for disabled, older
people and carers.

Tourism for All UK
c/o Vitalise
Shap Road Industrial Estate
Shap Road
Kendal
Cumbria
LA9 6NZ
Tel: 0845 124 9971
Fax: 0845 124 9972
Website: tourismforall.co.uk

Associations

There are many accommodation associations and groups
around the country that can offer you support when you are
setting up a new B&B. If you are a working farm, Farm Stay
UK, one of the largest such groups in England, may be a
useful organisation to contact.

Farm Stay UK Ltd
National Agricultural Centre
Stoneleigh Park
Warwickshire
CV8 2LG
Tel: 024 7669 6909
Fax: 024 7669 6630

Index